From Exchange to Contributions

From Exchange to Contributions

Generalizing Peer Production into the Physical World

Christian Siefkes

Version 1.01

October 2007

Edition C. Siefkes

Berlin

ISBN 978-3-940736-00-0

Published by Edition C. Siefkes,
Wilhelmshavener Str. 62, 10551 Berlin, Germany.

Printed by Lightning Source.

Website: http://www.peerconomy.org/

Contents

The world that we must seek is a world in which the creative spirit is alive, in which life is an adventure full of joy and hope, based rather upon the impulse to construct than upon the desire to retain what we possess or to seize what is possessed by others. It must be a world in which affection has free play, in which love is purged of the instinct for domination, in which cruelty and envy have been dispelled by happiness and the unfettered development of all the instincts that build up life and fill it with mental delights. Such a world is possible; it waits only for [wo]men to wish to create it.

Bertrand Russell, Roads To Freedom

1. Introduction

A new mode of production has emerged in the areas of software and content production during the last decades. This mode, which is based on sharing and cooperation, has spawned whole mature operating systems such as GNU/Linux and various BSD systems as well as innumerable other free software applications, some of which form the backbones of the Internet or the core of various enterprises; giant knowledge bases such as the Wikipedia; a large free culture movement often based on Creative Commons licenses; and a new, wholly decentralized medium for spreading, analyzing and discussing news and knowledge, the so-called blogosphere; among others.

Yochai Benkler has coined the term *peer production* to describe this collaborative and open mode of production which has become typical for the Internet in recent years (Benkler, 2002; 2006). Benkler makes it clear that *peer production* (or its generalization, *social production*) is a third mode of production that is fundamentally different from both *market*-based production and *firm* production. Market systems are based on *equivalent exchange* (with or sometimes without money), while firms (and also the former "socialist" planned economies such as the Soviet Union) rely on hierarchies and organized planning to distribute tasks and resources.

Peer production, on the other hand, is based on *contributions*. People contribute to a project because they want it to succeed, not because they need to earn money or have to realize some previously established plan. Some peer projects *require* contributions (peer-to-peer distribution networks such as BitTorrent require downloaders to upload), while others are open even to non-contributors (you do not have to write any free software to be allowed to use it). Often projects are partially, but not completely open; large free software and open content projects usually allow only active participants to take part in decision making processes, but everyone is allowed to access, distribute, and modify the produced information.

While Benkler has identified social production and peer production as important phenomena, he appears to consider them relevant only for certain niches of production, such as information goods. In this text we will discuss whether this limitation to niches—even important niches such as information goods—is justified or whether it under-estimates the potential of peer production. To put it in other words: Is a society possible in which peer production is the *primary* mode of production? If so, how could such a society be organized?

In the next two chapters, we will discuss several important characteristics of peer production and introduce the major problems that need to be addressed for generalizing peer production beyond the sphere of information. In Chapter 4 we will investigate how these problems can be addressed within the context of individual peer projects, finding that there are indeed suitable solutions. In Chapter 5 we will turn from the internal organization of peer projects to the "big picture," discussing how a multitude of such projects might fit together in a society where peer production is the primary mode of production.

Finding that such a society is feasible, we will in Chapter 6 compare it with societies based on market production and on planned production, the two economic modes that have been dominant during the last centuries. We will show that there are striking differences to both of them, and that a society based on peer production would grant people an unprecedented amount of control over their own lives, while avoiding the overhead, arbitrariness, or unfairness characteristic of other modes of production. Prior to concluding the text, we will examine how the people living in such a society might organize various aspects of their lives (Chap. 7), and we will address several concerns that might be brought forward in regard to such a *peer economy* (Chap. 8).

2. Elements of Peer Production

We will start our investigations by briefly treating some characteristic elements of the peer mode of production.

To prevent confusion about our use of the term *production* we would like to point out that we will use this term in a broad sense that can include any activities related to creating or doing something that is of use to anybody. *Production* in this sense comprises not just the design and manufacturing of new things, but also repair and maintenance, services of any kind, domestic work, etc.

Benkler differentiates between *peer production* and *social production,* regarding the former as a subset of the latter. We will not follow this distinction and use both terms largely synonymously.

2.1. Commons, Sharing, and Control over the Means of Production

Benkler uses the term *commons-based* peer production to describe the kind of peer production that has emerged on the Internet (free software, centralized or decentralized open content projects such as the Wikipedia and the blogosphere, distributed computing projects such as SETI@home, etc.). *Commons* are resources without owners who can control how they can be used; resources that are available to all who want to use them. The output of such peer projects generally becomes part of the commons, being freely available to everybody (or, at least, to everybody involved in the project).

In current peer projects, the resources required for these projects ("means of production" such as computing power and Internet access) are usually privately owned but readily available to all participants. Peer production thus fulfills the old Marxist postulate that *control over the means of production should be in the hands of the producers*: the means of production are available either as commons (peer projects can build upon the code and content produced by other projects) or as some kind of *pseudo-commons* (resources that are readily available to those who use them).

Information can be copied at almost zero cost, thus, being shared, it is still as available to the sharer as before. Some peer projects also involve the sharing of other resources which lack this property, but they do so in a pragmatic way which does not place a serious burden on the sharer. People participating in a wireless community network share their spurious networking capacity; the participants of shared computation projects such as SETI@home[1] donate computing power they don't need for any other purposes. This sharing philosophy might be expressed as "Share what you can"—sharing is commonplace, but nobody expects other people to give to others what they need for themselves. As Richard Stallman (2002, p. 46) puts it: "When I cook spaghetti, I do object if someone else eats it, because then I cannot eat it."

2.2. Free Cooperation

Cooperation is essential for many human activities—for all activities that cannot or are not handled by a single person. In a corporate or state context, cooperation usually contains an

[1] http://setiathome.berkeley.edu/

element of coercion—there is somebody who can tell you what to do, and then you should better do it, or else. . . .

In peer production, this moment of coercion is notably absent. Nobody can *order* others to do something, and nobody is forced to obey others. This does not mean that there are no structures—on the contrary, usually there are maintainers or admins or some other persons who can decide, for example, which contributions to accept and which to refuse. But nobody can compel others to do anything they do not want to do.

Moreover, all members of a project participate because of their own choice. You don't *have* to participate in a project, and there are no sanctions when you leave it.

Goals and internal organization of a project depend on the participants and will generally evolve along with a project. If some of the participants of a project are unhappy about some aspects of the project and cannot convince the others to change them, they can still *fork* the project: they can break away from the others and do their own thing.

Obviously, these traits of cooperation in a peer context cannot override the rules of the corporate world. In many large free software projects some of the development work is paid for by companies. For such paid developers, the normal rules of firms continue to apply—employees must obey their superiors, freelancers are bound to the contract they agreed to. But those who participate in a peer project without being paid for it, cooperate freely and are not subjected to anybody's command.

2.3. From Status to Reputation

In market economies (and also in planned economies such as the former Soviet Union), the *social position* and *social status* of a person tend to be important both as driving forces (people strive to increase their status) and as factors for judging others. In peer projects, *reputation* plays a similar role (cf. Lehmann, 2004).

Formal criteria such as job title or academic degree tend to be of little interest for peer projects; inborn characteristics, such as gender, "race," or age, are often not even known. Instead, people are judged by their contributions, and both the quality of contributions (developers writing good code) and the initiative of contributors (founding a new successful project) tend to increase a person's reputation.

Reputation is often more volatile than social status; it will suffer more quickly if people start misbehaving or making dubious or awkward contributions instead of helpful ones (this seems to have happened to Eric Raymond, a former star of the open source movement, at least to a certain degree). Project maintainers are expected to "do the right thing;" if the members of a project feel their decisions to be unfair or incompetent, they will sooner or later leave the project or start looking for a new maintainer.

Complementary to the decreased significance of social status, "status symbols," objects meant to imply a high social status of their owner, seem to lose importance. This is not surprising, since such symbols, which in a market economy usually indicate material wealth, can hardly indicate a person's *reputation.* Also, as stated above, peer production is largely centered around the concepts of *commons,* resources that are available to all; and where things are readily available for anyone who wants them, status symbols become rather pointless.

3. Problems to Solve for Generalization

After having quickly covered some of the traits we can observe for the current practice of peer production in the areas of software and content production, we will now turn to the problems that so far have limited the scope of this mode of production. There appear to be two fundamental problems that would need to be solved to generalize peer production into further areas of the physical world, beyond information production:

1. How to coordinate the producer side ("fun and passion") of peer production with the consumer side ("needs and desires")?
2. How to allocate limited resources and goods?

We will discuss each of these problems in turn.

3.1. How to Coordinate the Producer Side with the Consumer Side?

In any system of production and social organization, two roles of people can be distinguished: *producers* who create or provide goods (including services), and *consumers* who consume or use them. These two roles are not necessarily separate—people can be both producers and consumers at the same time ("prosumers"), but neither can they be expected to always fall together. Especially in regard to public services such as education, health care, and elder care, it is evident that the "consumers" of such services *cannot* generally be the same people that provide them.

Peer production, as we know it today, is mainly *producer-driven*: it relies on the choices and motivations of people acting as producers in what they want to produce. In many cases, these producers are also consumers (free software developers contribute to software they need or want to use), but people who *cannot* create what they want to use are generally out of luck; they cannot do much more than hope that somebody will pick up their needs.

This also affects the output of peer production processes—most free software programs, for example, are still far less user-friendly for the general public than proprietary programs; exceptions, such as the major Linux distributions, the Firefox browser and the Thunderbird e-mail client, or the OpenOffice suite, usually involve commercial players—they are partially driven by market forces, not pure examples of peer production.

Peer producers act out of fun, passion, and the desire to do something useful and to "give something back" to the community, as analyzed by Linus Torvalds and Pekka Himanen (Himanen, 2001) and by Lakhani and Wolf (2005), among others. They do what they do because they like doing it, because they love solving interesting problems, being creative, and creating something useful. Prosumers "scratch an itch," solving problems they wish to be solved in a way that is useful to others as well as to them, since in this way they are likely to get better results, by inciting others to contribute as well.

Such motivations will certainly remain fundamental driving forces, but peer production will hardly become the dominant mode of production unless there is a way to synchronize it with the other side of people—with people as users or consumers, people who have *needs* which they like to have satisfied even if they lack the knowledge or faculties to satisfy them themselves.

3.2. How to Allocate Limited Resources and Goods?

The second issue that needs to be addressed concerns the allocation and distribution of resources and goods that cannot be made available in sufficient amount to satisfy all needs. For information goods, this is not an issue, since (aside from legal obstacles) they can be copied as often as wished at practically zero cost. Material goods, however, are very different in this regard.

Personal fabricators, or *fabbers* (Gershenfeld, 2005), are an emergent technology that promises to make (at least some) material goods as easily and cheaply copyable as information goods. But while we can expect this technology to alleviate the problem of producing material goods at some point in the future, it will never fully solve it.

If peer production were only a viable option for *copyable* goods, generalizing it into the physical world would not be possible until fabbers have become sufficiently advanced. This might be the case in a few decades, or a few centuries, or maybe never. Even then, fabbers will need some resources to work, they will need to be produced and maintained, and they will hardly be able to produce *everything.* Hence, fabbers are unlikely to ever solve the problem of material production completely.

But let's assume that, at some point in the future, fabbers will be able to produce everything (including "big stuff" such as houses) without needing resources that are not already freely available to everyone. Even then, fabbers would not be able to solve all problems regarding material production and allocation. There are properties that cannot be copied, such as *location.* Even if fabbing were able to provide attractive apartments and houses for anyone who wants them, dwellings with sea view would remain a limited good, especially those that are near an attractive city center.

Rivalness is another problem regarding allocation that fabbers cannot solve—if everybody has their own car, nobody will get very far in it, because of all those jams. Then there are issues such as environmental damages caused by too many people using the same products. Clearly, while fabbing is an interesting technology that deserves attention, it will never become a "deus ex machina" able to solve all relevant problems.

4. Organizing Shared Production

Fabbing would allow an individual mode of production, where everybody would be able to produce what they need on their own, without the help of others. Without such an "autonomy" technology, people either have to rely on the market to buy what they need (assuming they can afford it), or else they need to cooperate with others, to jointly produce what they want to have, and to share and divide the results of this *shared production* process in a way that is acceptable to everyone involved.

People involved in shared production need to address several issues, which we will discuss in turn: they need to find others that are willing to cooperate; they need to find ways of obtaining sufficient contributions and ensuring that all required tasks are handled; and they have to find ways of assigning the produced results that are acceptable to everyone involved. In this chapter, we will regard these problems from the perspective of a single project; how to generalize the found solutions beyond this context will be discussed in the next chapter.

4.1. How to Find Others for Cooperation

There are two ways in which people tend to find other people for this process of cooperation: by common interest, or by location.

Finding others *by common interest* is the typical way in which the current Internet-based peer production processes tend to organize themselves: people contribute to free software programs they like or need; they write for the Wikipedia or other suitable forums about their topics of interest; they create and remix free music or other kinds of free culture in the styles and of the kinds they care about.

The alternative is finding others *by location*, i.e., cooperating with people in your neighborhood. This style of shared production is very old—it has probably been an element in the evolvement of social structures up from ancient times (cf. Sahlins, 1974, esp. pp. 74–95, 185–230).

The two alternatives do not exclude each other. There are peer projects where both interest and location matter, for example, book-sharing communities such as the Distributed Library Project[1].

In a society where shared production is the primary mode of production, we can expect both modes of finding others to be employed. There are things that concern all the people living in a specific area, such as the providing and maintenance of infrastructure, hence we may assume that everybody would be a member of a *local community* or some other kind of *local association* organizing these issues. And people with specific interests would continue to search others with similar interests and cooperate with them in the context of *peer projects*, just as they do now.

4.2. How to Obtain Contributions

As mentioned above, shared production is a very old mode of production; it has already figured in the lives of hunter-gatherer societies thousands of years ago. Since then, however,

[1] http://dlp.theps.net/

work has become more and more complex. Division of labor might not have been much of an issue in ancient societies, but it is essential for modern society.

In hunter-gatherer-style societies, what little specialization there was was usually assigned by *tradition*—tasks were distributed based on criteria such as gender (men were assumed to be hunters, women had to gather edible plants and to care for the children) or inheritance (the oldest son or child of a chief or shaman would become his successor). Obviously, such a tradition-based assigning of tasks would be unacceptable by modern standards; moreover, it would be completely insufficient to handle the complex division of labor we see today.

So how can peer projects and communities organize the internal division of labor; how can they ensure that all tasks are picked up?

Current peer projects usually rely on *voluntarism:* contributors choose a task or tasks they want to do among all open tasks (e.g., writing a new feature, fixing a bug, writing documentation, or testing, in case of a free software project); everybody contributes voluntarily as much (or as little) effort as they want.

Voluntarism is very reasonable for the production of certain goods, especially those that can be duplicated at near-zero cost, such as information goods—it would not make sense for the Wikipedia to exclude non-editors from reading articles. However, it is unclear how it should apply to the production of material goods where the production of additional units does cause additional non-trivial costs. A peer project aimed at producing cars (not just the design, but actual running vehicles) will hardly be able to hand over a car to everyone who wants one, whether they contribute anything or not—

even if the contributing members of the project were willing to do so, they would lack the necessary resources, so they will *have to* ask for some contribution in return.

Similarly, while *local communities* based entirely on voluntarism might be possible, it is hard to imagine that they would be stable. The organization of a community is very complex and involves a lot of tasks, not all of which are nice to do. There are tasks such as garbage removal which will probably be disagreeable to most people and are unlikely to draw sufficient volunteers.

Without volunteers, a community would fall into disarray; but even if some people volunteer for such disagreeable tasks, they would probably do so out of a sense of responsibility for the community, not because they like the task. This would lead to the risk of increased psychological strain within the community—the volunteers for the unpleasant jobs would most likely resent those who perform only agreeable tasks (or no tasks at all) and get away with it.

Peer projects and communities will therefore have to decide whether or not they *require* contributions from those who want to benefit from the cooperation (at least in regard to *material* benefits—information, as stated before, can be shared freely since sharing it does not cause additional cost). A simple way to do this would be to ask all participants to contribute a certain amount of hours (per month or some other suitable unit) to the project, letting contributors choose which tasks they want to handle. While such a *flat labor* approach might be suitable for some projects, it fails to address the observation made above: while people have widely different preferences about what they do and do not like, there are some tasks that nobody or almost nobody likes to do, because they are annoying, dirty, dangerous, or just plain boring.

If a project wants to be successful, it needs a way to cope

with such tasks, and generally to take people's preferences into account. In the next section we will discuss ways of doing this.

4.3. How to Ensure That Tasks Are Handled

There appear to be at least three strategies peer projects can use in regard to unpleasant tasks:

1. Automate them away;
2. Make them more fun (more agreeable, more interesting, safer, easier);
3. Make them shorter (by weighting them higher).

We suppose that all of these strategies would be employed in a society that relies primarily on peer production.

4.3.1. Automation

The power of automation has already shown amazing results during the last centuries. Various professions such as typesetters have become obsolete through the use of computers; in 1900, 38% of the U.S. labor force were occupied with farming; in 2000, this fraction had fallen below 3% (National Academy of Engineering, 2007); modern factories require only a small fraction of the labor of 18th century manufactories to produce items whose complexity would have been inconceivable even 50 years ago. There is little reason to assume that the possibilities of automation are already near a climax—more likely, it will continue to increase in the future, further reducing the amount of human work necessary to handle many tasks.

But in market-based systems, automation cannot reach its full potential especially in regard to unpleasant tasks. In market production, automation needs to be cost-efficient to be successful: the costs of introducing and using an automation technology must be lower (in the medium or long run) than the costs of the human labor it will supplant; otherwise companies that do not automatize will be able to produce cheaper than those that do and can thus expect more success in the marketplace (all other factors being equal). Hence, the lower paid a job is, the lower are the margins for successful automation. For reasons that are beyond the scope of this text, the unpleasant jobs are often ill-paid as well (think of garbage collectors or cleaners, for example). The market thus offers little incentives for automating them.

Shared production is very different in this regard—if all the members of a peer project want to avoid a specific task, they might spend considerable effort to get rid of it (or at least to reduce the amount or unpleasantness of the necessary work). Of course, they might also decide that it's not worth the trouble and instead agree on a mode of distributing the unpleasant work that's acceptable to all—but this decision will be up to them, depending only on their own preferences, not on market forces.

4.3.2. Fun

Another strategy that peer projects can use in dealing with unpleasant tasks that cannot (yet) be automated away is to make them more pleasant. There are many possibilities here that depend on the nature of the task: unsafe working conditions can be made safer; obnoxious work schedules can be abandoned (currently, office cleaners usually have to work very early or very late so as not to disrupt office work, but there are little reasons for peer projects to continue this practice); generally, many tasks can be made more fun, more interesting, more challenging than they are now—especially when those who do the task decide on how to do it, as is normal for peer projects.

Again, the options of peer projects in this regard extend far beyond what is possible on the market. In markets, the lowest bidder usually wins, so corporations will generally be unable to take any measure for making working conditions safer or more enjoyable that would increase the cost of production unless their competitors are forced to follow (e.g., by law). And corporations have little incentive to make working conditions more attractive as long as they find sufficient applicants desperate even for bad jobs. Peer producers, however, do not have to underbid their competition; they have both the incentive and the means to make their work more agreeable.

4.3.3. Weighted Labor (Task Auctioning)

While automation and fun are ways of lightening the tasks that the members of a peer project have to handle, they don't yet solve the problem posed in Section 3.1: they don't bring the consumer side of the members of a project (who want certain tasks to be done) in accord with their producer side (who prefer doing certain tasks over doing others). If every member of a project chooses freely their preferred tasks (producer side) among all available tasks (consumer side), the sum of all those independent producer decisions is unlikely to match the summed preferences of the consumer side; in general, some tasks will attract more volunteers than necessary, while there won't be enough volunteers for other tasks.

It would be possible to solve this problem through mechanisms such as "first come, first serve" (if there are more applicants than needed for a certain tasks, those that applied last will have to choose again among the less popular tasks) or drawing lots. However, such proposals don't sound very attractive. They would mean that some people end up doing what they really want to do, while others have to content themselves with their second choices (or worse), just because of bad luck or because they didn't hurry enough.

Is there a better way? Can the members of a peer project find a way of matching their collective preferences as producers with their collective preferences as consumers that allows everyone to choose which tasks they prefer to do and still ensures that all the required tasks will actually get done?

To answer this question, we need to realize that there is another dimension in regard to which preferences differ: *time.* People's preferences vary not just in regard to the tasks they like to do, but also in regard to the time they are willing to spend for a project. An unpleasant task gets more pleasant if it takes a shorter amount of somebody's time, giving them more time to pursue other interesting projects, to socialize with or make love to other people, or just be lazy. If I have to decide whether I prefer spending the same amount of time on a task I like more (say, writing software) or one I like less (say, removing garbage), it won't take me long to choose the former. But if the question is whether I spend 20 hours a week writing software or five hours a week removing garbage, I'm likely to have second thoughts (cf. Fig. 4.1).

Computers make it easy to automatically match people's preferences along these two dimensions (their producer preferences) with the tasks they want to have handled (their consumer preferences). A peer project can set up a *task auctioning* system where the participants can choose the tasks they prefer doing among all available tasks. Tasks that don't attract sufficient volunteers are then weighted higher (i.e., people picking them up will have to do less work for the project) until there are enough people willing to accept the time/task trade-off. Similarly, tasks which are more popular than necessary are weighted lower, so the people who want to do them will have to reconsider whether they prefer spending more time with

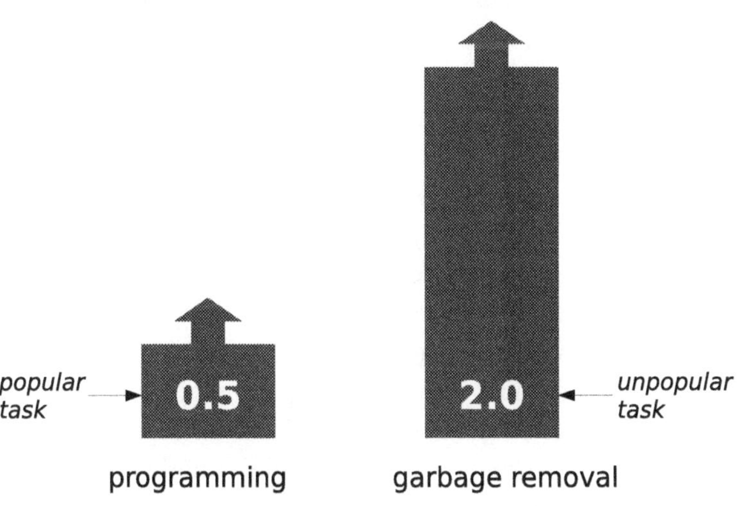

Figure 4.1.: Weighted labor

this task or whether there isn't another task they also like doing that gives them more time for other activities.

Thus, a *weighted hour* of labor could be used as unit for measuring contributions. During a month or a year, all the members of a project (except those who are exempted from contributing, cf. Sec. 8.1.1) will be expected to contribute the same amount of *weighted hours*—the amount that is necessary to ensure that all tasks have been handled. Depending on the tasks people choose to do, this equal amount of weighted hours will correspond to an amount of actually worked hours that might be considerably higher (for very popular tasks) or lower (for unpopular tasks).

Such a task auctioning mechanism is a way to ensure that all relevant tasks are handled, while at the same time allowing everybody to freely choose the activities they prefer; nobody is forced into doing or not doing certain things. It takes care not only of unpleasant tasks, but also of tasks that require special talents or skills that only few people possess. Provided there is more demand for such tasks than volunteers able to do them, they will automatically be weighted higher, increasing the motivation for people with the required talents to use them rather than do something everybody else could do as well.

There are many variations in how exactly such a system can be realized. Projects might choose to set an upper limit for the weights of tasks. If some tasks reach this upper limit and remain unassigned, the project members will have to decide how to proceed: they could choose to raise the limit; they could agree to distribute such unpopular tasks evenly among all participants so everybody will have to do their share of them now and then; in some cases they might just decide to do without them. Similarly, projects might choose to impose lower limits for the weights and use other procedures to decide if there are still too many applicants for such tasks (such as "first come, first serve," drawing lots, "job" interviews, or elections).

Generally, just because a person *wants* to do something does not mean that others will trust them to do it well, hence not every contribution somebody is willing to provide will be accepted by the peer project (just like today's peer projects don't automatically accept any contributions). We will discuss this issue in Section 8.1.3.

A large part, but not all of the contributions required for shared production are labor, but to figure out how non-labor resources can be brought into a project we need to see the big picture. This will happen in Chapter 5. Those who are interested in the gory mathematical details of the auctioning mechanisms proposed in this text will find them in the appendix (A).

4.4. How to Assign Results of a Project

4.4.1. Share What You Can

We have seen above (Sec. 2.1) that peer production is characterized by an approach to sharing that is both generous and pragmatic. People will generally share what they can without suffering a serious loss, but there is no pressure to relinquish what you want to use yourself.

We can assume that this practice of generously sharing what can easily be shared will continue, there being no indications to the contrary. Peer projects will probably continue to share non-personal information (where there are no privacy concerns) with the members of other projects and the general public without imposing serious restrictions.

The one restriction that is frequent in current peer production is to require that modified versions also stay in the commons (*share-alike* or *copyleft* clause); another restriction that is seldom applied to software, but more often to content is to forbid others from using shared information for purposes of market production (*non-commercial* clause). These restrictions are imposed by some peer projects but not by others, and we can expect this mixed attitude toward them to continue into the future.

The *non-commercial* restriction would become irrelevant in an economic system where peer production is the *only* mode of production, but not earlier. The *share-alike* condition will always remain significant since it grants any users a right to access and use the *source code* (the preferred form of a work for making modifications to it) of modified versions of a work—an option that they might not have otherwise, since people could decide to modify a work and distribute their modified version only in binary form (unsuitable for further modification).

4.4.2. But What About the Rest?

Generally, sharing does not scale quite as efficiently as the sharing of information. A spaghetti-cooking project will hardly be able to share the output of their activities with everybody who wants spaghetti; when in doubt, they will prefer to eat the cooked spaghetti themselves instead of staying hungry. So, the contributors to a peer project producing something that cannot easily be shared with everybody else will often share only among themselves.

In which ways can they organize this internal sharing?

We will discuss several possible modes. These modes do not necessarily conflict with each other and can be combined. Which of these modes makes most sense depends on what is produced and on the preferences of the prosumers.

4.4.2.1. Flat Rates

The spaghetti-cooking group points to one obvious answer to the sharing problem: most likely they will not put any specific restrictions on how much spaghetti a group member may eat. Instead, while every participant will be expected to contribute in some way or other to cooking the food and organizing the dinner, all the contributors are allowed to eat how much or how little they like, until the spaghetti is all used up. Dinners or parties of friends are often organized in this way, reminding us that social production is nothing new but has been with us, though largely invisible, for a long time.

We will refer to this model as the *flat rate* model since it resembles the flat pricing schemas that have become popular for broadband Internet access and (at least in some countries) for phone calls. In other domains, different names such as "all-inclusive" travel and "All you can eat" restaurants are used for what is essentially the same phenomenon; public transportation services often offer monthly or yearly tickets for a flat fee.

In a market-based economy these models have in common that a single fixed fee is charged for a service, regardless of actual usage. For the provider, such flat pricing models are often easier to manage than more fine-grained accounting mechanisms; for the users they are often cheaper and, in any case, more convenient, since the exact costs are known in advance.

In peer production, the equivalent model means that a flat amount of contributions is required and that everybody who contributes sufficiently to a peer project can choose freely from the results of the project.

4.4.2.2. Flat Allocation

Let us turn from the spaghetti-cooking group to other peer projects. How could, for example, a car-producing project allocate the produced items? A project that is building actual, physical cars, not just the design of a car (as is the goal of the OScar[2] and c,mm,n[3] projects)?

Probably they wouldn't be very happy with a flat rate model where everybody contributes a roughly equal amount but then takes one, two, or any number of the produced cars, just as they like. Some of those who would need only a single car (probably the large majority) would be annoyed about having to work more so *others* can take more cars; they might be tempted to take more cars than they actually need to make up for it or to save for the future. Some people would take more cars than they need for themselves and give them to friends who haven't contributed anything to the project. Bad feelings, or worse, would result.

The project can avoid this problem by choosing a *flat allocation* model instead of a flat rate model: everybody will get just one car (instead of any number of cars) for a certain amount of contributions. Those who want two cars will have to contribute twice as much, and so on. This also removes any reasons for mistrust whether participants are producing for themselves or for others; they can donate the produced items to their friends without harming or annoying anyone else in the project.

This flat allocation model, where everybody gets a produced unit (e.g., a car) for a certain amount of contributions, will be especially appropriate for the production of discrete items

[2] http://www.theoscarproject.org/

[3] http://www.autoindetoekomst.nl/website/

(such as cars or computers) where all the produced items are roughly equivalent in terms of production effort.

4.4.2.3. Customized Production and Preference Choice (Production Effort)

What if things become more complicated than either a flat rate or a flat allocation model can handle? Think, for example, on the question of *housing.* Not all houses and apartments are created equal, and there is no way in which this could be "fixed" (think of sea view). Nor, actually, is there a reason why it should be "fixed"—some people might prefer large luxurious houses and might be ready to put a large effort into getting them; others might be happy with smaller or simpler apartments, preferring to spend their time and effort for other purposes.

A peer project or community organizing housing for its members will need to take variety in the produced items (houses or apartments) as well as the differing preferences of its members into account. "One size fits all" won't do it.

A partial answer comes from the fact that the relative *production efforts* that are required for the production of various items will be known, especially if a *weighted labor* model of task distribution is used (cf. Sec. 4.3.3). This allows a peer project to customize its production according to the wishes of each participant, even when such custom-made products require a production effort that is higher or lower than the average—in such cases, the respective participants will probably be expected to make contributions that are accordingly higher or lower. She who wants a larger and more luxurious house can have it if she is ready to contribute more to make up for the higher production effort (measured, e.g., in weighted hours) that goes into building and maintaining it.

Similarly, while a peer project providing various foodstuffs for its members might choose a *flat rate* model for many normal foods (since nobody can eat that much more or less than other people), it might use such a *preference choice* model for more sumptuous or luxurious items such as whiskey or caviar. In such a case, "normal" participants (who contribute just as much as everybody else) might be able to choose freely from among such "luxury goods" up to a certain amount; while those who want more of them will be expected to make accordingly higher contributions.

4.4.2.4. Preference Weighting (Product Auctioning)

Preference choice alone might not work in all cases. We already mentioned the "sea view" example—a dwelling with sea view won't take a higher production effort than one without. Some people might not care, but, when given the choice, more people might prefer dwellings with sea view than available in any seaside community (inland communities will have similar problems in other areas). Customized production cannot help here since coastlines cannot be extended at will.

One way to decide between such overlapping preferences in a fair and non-arbitrary way is to introduce a *preference weighting* (product auctioning) mechanism that is similar to the weighted labor (task auctioning) model discussed above. If there is more demand for any given product than can be satisfied, a peer project can raise the relative cost (the amount of required contributions) of this product until sufficiently many of the prospective users get second thoughts *(upward auctioning).* Conversely, if there is something available that nobody wants to have, the project can make it more attractive by lowering its relative costs *(downward auctioning).* Note that "product" here denotes anything that has been *produced* by a project—this includes services just as well as material goods.

Of course, a peer project will generally try to accommodate its production to the existing internal demand as well as possible; but whenever this is not possible (e.g., due to the limited availability of "natural resources" such as sea view), this preference weighting model can make up for it. As in the case of the task auctioning system, such a *product auctioning* mechanism can be conveniently designed as a computerized system.

Note that it is the *relative* cost that is modified—if the relative cost (amount of contributions) for one specific item is increased, the relative costs of all other items will automatically fall. After all, the whole effort necessary to fulfill the goals of a peer project is just *distributed* among its members—a project needs to ensure that all tasks are picked up, but, beyond that, "there is nothing left to do" (within the limits of the project), so people can and will spend their remaining time and energy in other ways.

Both the weighted labor model and this preference weighting model ensure that everybody's preferences have free play. Nobody is forced to do a task they do not really want to do or to live in conditions they don't really like. You can freely choose whether you prefer more *luxury* (and of which kinds) or more *laziness;* whether you prefer spending more time doing the things you want to do, or working for the things you want to have, or whether you prefer living in a simple style or doing some "quick-and-dirty" tasks so you can spend most of your time in wholly other ways.

Of course, if you want luxury of all kinds *and* a life of idleness that doesn't involve any activities which are useful to others, you might be out of luck—unless you can convince others to provide everything for you. In general, you will have to make a decision that involves some kind of trade-off. But this decision will be based on your own free choices; it won't be made for you by other people, nor by luck or fate (say, based on lot, or the income or social position your parents happen to have).

Figure 4.2 depicts the four different allocation models we have covered.

4.4.2.5. Usage vs. Ownership

We have discussed the example of housing. Let's take a look at what the products of such a project will actually be. Will it be the actual houses or apartments built by the project, to be used by the respective inhabitants for as long as they want and then to be disposed of in any way they choose? This might be a possibility, but only if there is a *market* for people to get rid of dwellings they no longer need. Otherwise people who only need housing for a limited period of time would be put at a serious disadvantage: they would have to contribute just as much as if they wanted to live there "forever."

Is there a way in which peer production can solve this problem without having to rely on a complementary market system? The answer is obvious when we remember the flat rate model discussed above. With flat rates, a certain amount of contributions is required for a given time of usage, say, a month of Internet access. The same model can be used for housing: contributions are required for living in a dwelling for a certain amount of time, not for living there forever. For each new month or year you stay there, you will have to make additional contributions; if you no longer need the dwelling, you will give it back to your local community (cf. Sec. 4.1—housing might be managed most suitably by local communities or associations, since houses are bound to a specific location).

Flat Rate:

Effort is shared evenly among all

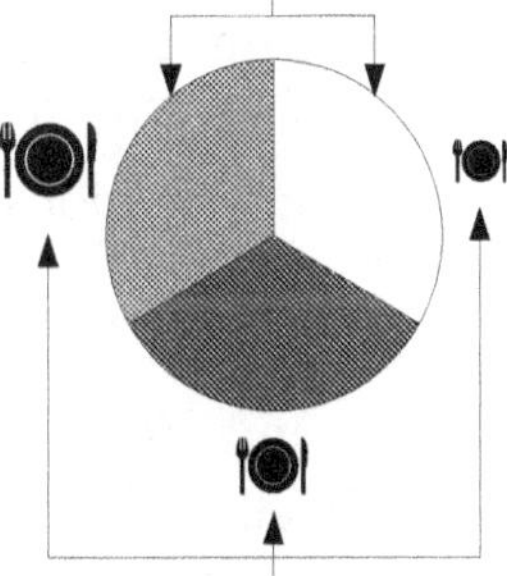

Everybody takes as much as they like

Flat Allocation:

Everybody contributes the same...

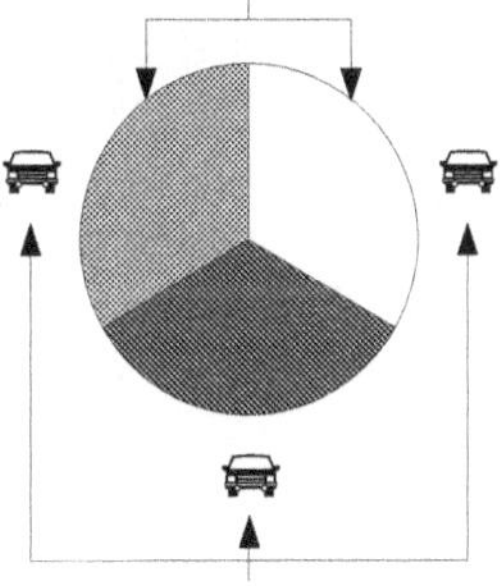

...to get one unit

Production Effort:

Everyone contributes the amount of effort...

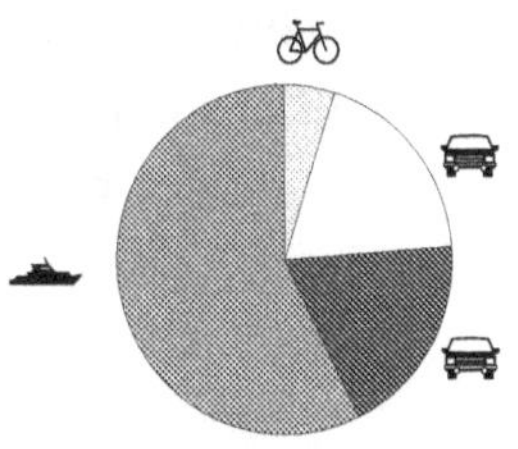

...required to produce the goods they like to have

Preference Weighting:

Required effort is adjusted until demand matches supply:

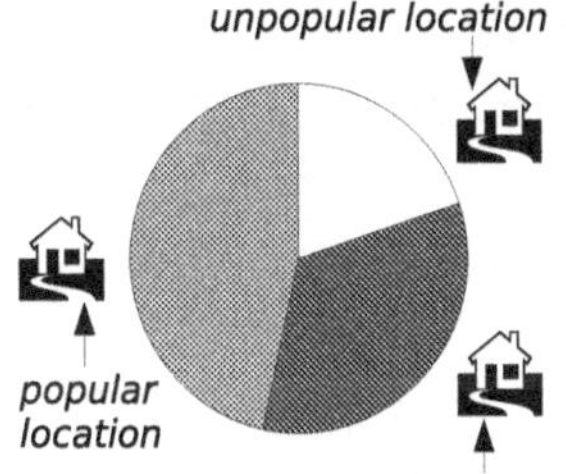

- For popular goods you contribute more effort than required for production
- For unpopular goods less

Figure 4.2.: Effort sharing models for non-copyable goods

The community will then give the dwelling to somebody else willing to make the necessary contributions.

We can therefore expect housing in a peer production–based economy to be more similar to renting than to buying a dwelling in a market system; the main difference being that there is no separate person or corporation you are renting it from; instead, you get it from your own local community. The produced dwellings can be considered a part of the commons—they are commonly owned by the community, which makes them available to its members on a for-use basis.

Again, there is no need that contributors and users are actually identical. Somebody can inhabit a dwelling herself, share it with her family and/or her friends, or just give it to friends; this does not matter as long as she is willing to make the necessary contributions.

Such an allocation system that is based on usage (possession) instead of ownership (property) might be appropriate in other situations as well. Whenever the expected "lifespan" of a given product exceeds the expected time of usage by any given person, a usage-based system seems reasonable, since it avoids generating unnecessary garbage (still good things being thrown away because the original user no longer needs them) and does not depend on a secondary market for used things.

5. Fitting It All Together: A Peer Economy

In the last chapter we discussed the issues that arise in regard to the internal organization of any given peer project. Now we are ready to turn from this internal view to the "big picture." A society based primarily on peer production would comprise a multitude of such projects. How will they fit together? How will they make decisions and how will they resolve conflicts? How will they allocate resources? In short, how can we expect such a *peer economy* to work?

5.1. Society as a Big Project or a Multitude of Projects

Considering the generalization of peer production from a single peer project to a whole society, there are two complementary views of such a society we may take: Society can be considered as a *multitude of peer projects*, each deciding on its goals and its internal organizing. But society can also be considered as a kind of *big project* (very big, indeed), where mechanisms for sharing efforts and assigning produced goods (such as discussed in the last chapter) are applied to society at large.

We suppose that, to understand how the people living in such a society will organize their lives, both these views have some validity—neither of them would be sufficient in isolation, but together they might give us a good picture. A society based primarily on peer production *will* comprise a multitude of projects; but between them, the people involved in these projects are likely to establish some institutions that will make society itself—or some smaller or larger parts of it—resemble a big project in some ways. In the following sections, we will look at several reasons for such cooperation beyond projects, and discuss the forms it may take.

5.2. Sharing Effort Between Projects: Distribution Pools

To understand a first aspect of where the "society as a big project" view makes sense, we have to remember the problem of how to coordinate the producer side of people with their consumer side (discussed in Sec. 3.1). As consumers, people generally have many diverse needs and desires. Having to contribute to lots of different peer projects each specializing in satisfying one or a few of them—one project for housing, other ones for food, clothing, body care, electric gadgets, games and toys, books and magazines, etc.—would clearly be very impractical, if not infeasible.

But to organize a single project that produces lots of different goods to satisfy all or most of the needs of its members (in so far as they can be regarded as problems of production) does not sound like a convincing solution either. Since a project needs some decision-making structures to decide what to produce and how to produce it, such a huge project might become quite ponderous and bureaucratic. And since different people have different needs, it would always produce goods that some of its members don't care about, while not producing goods that other members would like to have.

Therefore people will probably prefer a middle way, with different specialized projects all setting their goals and deciding on their internal organization separately, but sharing tasks and results as if they were a single huge project. They can do so by using a *single shared system* for distributing both the *tasks* they need to have handled and the *results* of their cooperation (the goods they have produced). Tasks and products can be distributed in the same way as before—using task auctioning (cf. Sec. 4.3.3) to assign tasks and allocation based on production effort or preference weighting to distribute non-copyable products (cf. Sec. 4.4.2)—but among all the participants of such a *distribution pool* instead of just the members of a single project.

This would allow everyone participating in a distribution pool to benefit from results produced by *any* of the aggregated projects. You do not have to work for lots of different projects to get all the various things you need or like to have. As long as there are projects producing the desired items in your distribution pool, you only contribute your part of the required effort to the pool, doing tasks of your choice for one or a few of the participating projects until the amount of weighted labor necessary for the products you desire has been reached (as determined by the task and product auctioning system).

Organizing a joint task and product auctioning system for a distribution pool will be slightly, but not essentially, more complicated than organizing such a system for a single project. One additional factor which might be irrelevant for single projects is the *location* where tasks are to be performed. Since people might be willing to do a certain task but unwilling to move to a different place for doing so, it is quite likely that some labor (working as a baker or as a medical doctor, say) will be weighted higher in one town and lower in other places. The project for which a task is to be handled is another factor that will sometimes influence task popularity, since many people will prefer working for projects with a high *reputation* (cf. Sec. 2.3) and will shy away from projects whose reputation is bad. Projects that are perceived as "doing the wrong thing," say, by treating their contributors badly, by producing goods of dubious quality, or by engaging in activities that harm the environment, will tend to get negative reputation which will make it more difficult for them to attract contributors.

Efforts spent for the production of goods that have to be distributed via *downward auctioning* (cf. Sec. 4.4.2.4) probably won't be recognized fully, but only partially (proportional to the downward auctioning), as contributions to a distribution pool. Downward auctioning indicates that nobody considers these goods "worth the effort." If a pool would nevertheless recognize the whole production effort, it would allow projects to produce things that nobody wants and in return get access to other goods, without having contributed anything useful by themselves. Note that it will still be possible to acquire goods for less effort than required (and recognized) for producing them, since *upward auctioning* of some goods automatically reduces the effort necessary to get all the others. (Cf. Sec. A.2 in the mathematical appendix for more on this problem and its solution.)

The larger a distribution pool becomes, the better for the participants, since any additional projects increase their choices, both in regard to the tasks to perform and the produced items to select from. Ideally, a single global distribution pool will emerge, comprising *all* the projects that are interested in pooling. Such a huge pool would not pose a risk of centralization or of concentration of power, since the pool itself would only be a passive piece of software. All the participating projects would still decide for themselves what they produce and how they organize their activities.

It is important to realize that for most people, contributions will just take the form of doing some of the things they prefer doing. No one will be forced to spend time with activities they don't like, aside from doing their chosen work, except in the unusual case that none of the projects they prefer working with should be ready to accept their contributions.

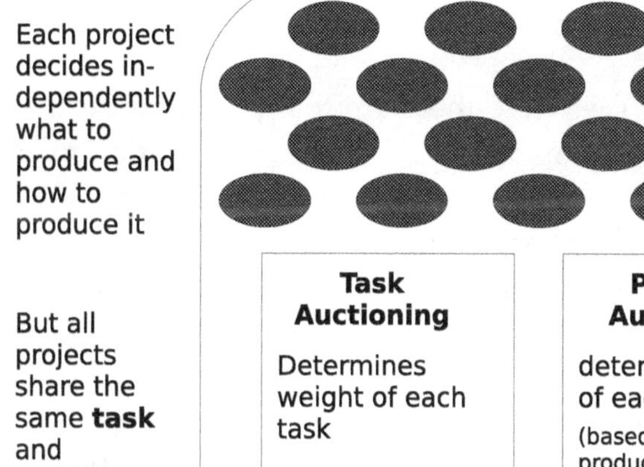

Figure 5.1.: Distribution pools

Figure 5.1 illustrates the core ideas of the distribution pool model.

5.3. Organizing Infrastructure and Public Services: Local Associations

As stated before (Sec. 4.1), there are things that concern all the people living in a specific area: the organization of infrastructure and of public services such as health care, child and elder care, education, and protection and aid in case of emergencies or trouble (emergency services, fire fighting, etc.). This is another aspect for which the "multitude of projects" view is insufficient. Without some coordination among the concerned, the likely result would either be chaos (with the activities of different projects conflicting with each other) or else stagnation (with nobody providing such services since everybody waits for others to make the necessary effort).

While any such activities can be handled by specific projects, the people living in an area need to find a way of *coordinating* them to avoid chaos. And to avoid stagnation, they will have to *share the required effort* among themselves in a way that is acceptable to all. They can do both by founding a *local meta-project* that coordinates these issues and distributes the effort.

We use the term "meta-project" since it would not be necessary to found a separate project that organizes infrastructure and public services all by itself. Instead, there will probably be various peer projects organizing different tasks (a project building and maintaining streets and bridges, another one running a hospital, a third organizing a fire brigade, etc.), and it would be up to the meta-project to coordinate them and to make sure that they all operate as expected.

Since the scales most suitable for organizing a task vary for different tasks, we may assume that everybody will be not just a member of a single *local meta-project* (or *local association*), but of several local meta-projects of different sizes that nest into each other. We will explore this issue in Section 5.3.2.

5.3.1. Which Services to Organize and How to Make Them Available

A core issue which the members of such a *local association* will have to decide is which services they choose to organize and which of the various allocation models discussed in Section 4.4 they choose for making them available.

We wouldn't be surprised if they will often decide to take a comprehensive approach to the organization of *infrastructure,* providing not only streets but also public transportation systems; not only access to water, electricity, and energy, but also communication channels such as postal services, telephone and Internet; sewage and garbage disposal will obviously be necessary too. Granting access on a *flat rate* basis will probably be most suitable for many of these items; though local associations might prefer accounting based on *production effort* and *preference weighting* for some areas (say water or energy) if wasteful usage turns out to be a problem or if they desire to reduce usage due to its environmental impact.

For *public services,* flat rate allocation often seems a matter of fairness. People don't generally *choose* to become ill or frail, so it would be unfair to expect them to contribute more because of a choice they did not make. Actually, people who need care because they are too old to care for themselves will generally be unable to make up for it with any contributions, so flat rate accounting is the only real option here.

Similarly, flat rate accounting seems most fair when it comes to education and learning, especially for children. Quite likely, children—similar to old people—won't even be expected to contribute *anything* (cf. Sec. 8.1.1), so they themselves cannot make up for it. There is little reason why it should be specifically the parents who have to contribute more to allow their children to learn, and it would hardly be justifiable to prevent children from learning if their parents are unwilling or unable to make up for it.

We suppose that local associations will tend to consider the acquisition of knowledge or skills as a contribution, sparing learners the necessity to contribute to the local meta-project in other ways, at least to a certain degree. Since communities and regions benefit if their inhabitants can handle a wide variety of tasks in a skillful way, it only makes sense for them to encourage people to broaden their horizon and improve their skills.

Organization of housing is another issue that is best handled at the local level, as mentioned above (Sec. 4.4.2.5). We suppose that customized production and preference weighting will be the most appropriate models here.

Of course, the people living in a specific area will never be limited to the offerings coordinated by their local meta-projects—they can always join or organize independent peer projects to provide alternatives.

5.3.2. Levels of Local Cooperation

5.3.2.1. Communal Meta-Projects (Local Communities)

How many people might join forces in such local associations? People will find out suitable sizes by themselves, but we can already make some conjectures.

While (as stated above) we wouldn't be surprised if *distribution pools* become very large, we don't think the same will happen with local meta-projects. Since the local situation will be somewhat different from area to area, smaller meta-projects will be able to cope more flexibly with their local situation.

Also, local meta-projects will need to make decisions about which services to provide and how to organize them; and the larger a meta-project is, the smaller the role of each individual member in the decision-making processes becomes. In a meta-project with millions of members, people might feel as if they "don't matter" for the workings of the project and as if they have little chance to influence its decisions.

On the other hand, meta-projects that are too small will have problems coordinating all the tasks they want to handle—the various activities outlined above will need a high degree of division of labor and specialization to fill all the required roles. Also, many activities will be difficult or inefficient to organize if there aren't enough potential "customers" (e.g., health care beyond the most basic level). For these reasons we suppose that meta-projects of a few 10,000 people (or less) would not run quite smoothly—they might be better off if they unite with others to form a larger group.

Local communities (or *peer communities*) of about 100,000 to 500,000 people might be of a better size to organize a local meta-project—neither too small to flexibly organize manifold tasks, nor too large to stay in tune with the daily lives of their members. Thus the people living in a medium-sized town, or a quarter of a larger city, or a group of villages or small towns, could cooperate to organize a *communal meta-project.*

5.3.2.2. Large-scale Cooperation at the Regional Level and Beyond

Resources such as electricity can often be most efficiently produced on a large scale. And there are physical items of which each local community will only need a few, say, trams or buses for their public transportation system, construction machinery for building streets and houses, or specialized equipment, for example for hospitals.

We can expect local communities to cooperate with adjacent communities to handle efforts that require coordination beyond the communal level, organizing in a *regional meta-project* such tasks and services that cannot efficiently be organized at the communal level. *Regions* (or *peer regions*) comprising about 30 to 50 local communities might be of a good size for such purposes—they would be large enough (about 3 to 15 million people) to address most efforts for which a single community is too small, and yet small enough to ensure that all the involved communities and their members have a say in the decisions regarding the regional level.

Such cooperation is especially reasonable for the organization of transport systems between communities and for other large-scale infrastructure projects. Groups of neighboring communities will also tend to cooperate in regard to the building and running of universities and research institutes, opera houses and museums, specialized medical centers, and other institutions that would strain the capacities of a single community.

We suppose that such regions of several million people will be large enough for most purposes. If and when they are not, regions can cooperate with other regions at the *superregional* level, in a similar way to local communities cooperating at the regional level. Finally, such large *superregions* (which might comprise about 30 to 50 regions with 150 to 500 million inhabitants, assuming a similar jump in scale) can cooperate with each other at the *global* level. Global cooperation might make sense for the organization of very large research activities such as space exploration or particle physics.

5.3.2.3. Small-scale Cooperation and Neighborhoods

Structures that are far smaller than a single local community will continue to matter as well. Many people will live in *households* with friends or family, like today. *Groups of households* might pool together their use of resources that each of them needs occasionally but not all the time, such as washing machines, specialized kitchen equipment, or toolboxes; and they might help each other regarding the organization of day-to-day activities such as child care. Such kinds of sharing and cooperation are nothing new, but they will probably be more frequent and commonplace in a peer economy, which is centered around possession and cooperation, than in a market-based economy, which is based on private property and on buying and selling.

Of course, there is no reason to suppose that shared usage will be obligatory. People will be free to decide whether they prefer the shared usage of an item (such as a washing machine) or whether they prefer to have their own. Either decision will have some advantages and some disadvantages—sharing something will require some coordination and you might sometimes have to wait until it becomes available, but using your own will require a higher effort to get and to maintain it, and you might need additional room for storage.

In addition to and beyond such small-scale cooperation which will probably be largely *ad hoc,* people might establish *commons centers* to facilitate sharing and cooperation on a somewhat larger and more organized scale, say among five hundred to a few thousand people (a *neighborhood,* or *peer neighborhood*). Such a *commons center* could comprise specialized equipment and tools, a car pool, a small library, and a party room, and whatever else people prefer to share. It could also serve as a meeting point and as organizational basis for the shared handling of day-to-day activities.

Figure 5.2 resumes the approximate scales and main purposes of the various levels of local associations proposed in this model.

5.3.3. Ensuring That Tasks Are Handled

The people living together in a local association will not only have to decide which kinds of infrastructure and public services they want to organize, but they will also need ways of distributing the necessary tasks among themselves. The most flexible way of doing so is by participating with the respective local meta-project in a *distribution pool* (cf. Sec. 5.2). Due to the effort-balancing effect of distribution pools, this means that the members of a local association will have to contribute as much effort to the pool as they take out of it: together, they need to contribute enough weighted labor to the distribution pool to make up for the overall effort required for the activities coordinated by their local meta-project. But since distribution pools use a shared task auctioning system for all participating projects, they can do this by contributing to any project in the pool—they do not necessarily have to contribute to projects coordinated by the local meta-project.

For infrastructure and public services made available on a *flat-rate* basis, this means that the required effort will be distributed evenly among everyone who benefits, i.e., among all the inhabitants of the respective local association (except those who are exempted, cf. Sec. 8.1.1). For example, if the tasks a local community decides to organize on a flat-rate basis take one million weighted hours a week and there are 200,000 contributing members, each community member will have to contribute five weekly hours of weighted labor to the distribution pool (to any project or projects of their choice).

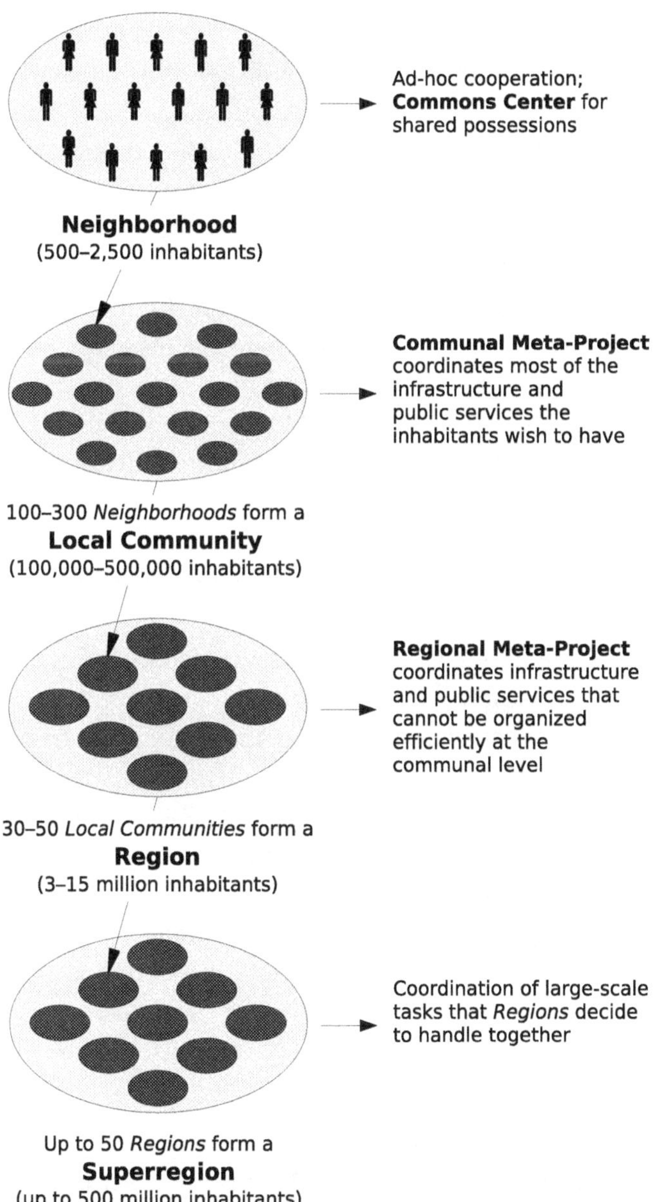

Figure 5.2.: Sizes and purposes of local associations

While participation in other peer projects is by choice, participation in local meta-projects will probably be automatic. By moving in any given area you agree that you are willing to take your part in contributing to the effort it takes to organize infrastructure and public services that your local association decides to handle on a flat-rate basis since they potentially concern all or most people. At least this seems to be a reasonable assumption, since the alternative—that people decide for themselves whether they want to have health care and protection from calamities such as fires etc.—doesn't fly. It would mean that if you suffer an accident or a severe illness or if your house burns down, the others either will have to stand by without helping or they will have to help without getting anything in return. The first option is hardly conceivable, which means that you cannot really opt out from using such services.

Thus, expecting everyone to take their share in organizing them seems just fair: since opting out from *using* such public services is not feasible, we suppose that opting out from *organizing* them won't be feasible either. The same holds for the organization of at least some kinds of infrastructure: everyone will like to use the streets now and then, everyone will benefit from having access to water and electricity and from having working sewage and garbage disposal systems.

Remember that this does not mean that anybody will be forced to participate in any specific activity; most people will contribute their share in weighted hours by doing one of their preferred activities.

5.4. Coordinating Production: Prosumer Associations

A third aspect in which we expect the *free cooperation* characteristic for peer production (cf. Sec. 2.2) to transcend the limits of a single project concerns the coordination of production and the sharing of experiences and knowledge among projects active in the same sector of production. If we regard local associations as coordinating production processes *vertically* among people and projects from a specific area, we can consider such cooperation between projects active in the same sector of production as *horizontal* coordination. We will use the term *prosumer association* to refer to any institutions (formal or informal) facilitating such horizontal coordination among the people and projects involved as producers or consumers (or both) in a specific sector of production.

We will now investigate several forms which such coordination may take, discussing for each form whether and why it is likely to occur.

5.4.1. Adjusting Supply to Demand

An important goal that projects can reach by coordinating their activities is to *better adjust supply to demand,* by projects coordinating which and how many goods they produce. This only affects projects that address the same set of consumers, say projects distributing their products in the same *distribution pool.*

From the viewpoint of producing projects, the main risk that can be reduced by such coordination is *overproduction:* if they don't coordinate their production, they risk producing more goods than consumers want to have. For producers, the risk here is *wasted effort:* if they produce a good that nobody wants to have, the effort they spent producing it will have been totally wasted; if they only manage to distribute a good via *downward auctioning,* the effort will only be recognized in part (cf. the remark in Sec. 5.2 regarding downward auctioning in distribution pools). In either case, they would have been better off spending their time for producing something which is actually needed (either by themselves or by somebody else). For producers, it clearly makes sense to coordinate their activities with other projects working on similar goods, since they cannot be sure in advance whether it would be them or others whose effort will have been wasted if they produce too much (if all their products are of comparable quality, the likely result is that they will all be distributed via downward auctioning, so all the projects would suffer).

For the consumer side, *underproduction* is the more serious risk. In many cases, underproduction will be easily noticeable by products being distributed via *upward auctioning*, i.e., for more effort than necessary for producing them (cf. Sec. 4.4.2.4); additionally, prosumer associations can also keep *wish lists* to collect "feature requests" for products and features that are not yet produced. These indicators will give people and projects looking for worthwhile tasks hints about where to start.

In a peer economy, there is at least no risk of *dedicated* underproduction. Market producers might and will produce less than they could if this allows them to increase their profits by getting higher prices. Peer producers, on the other hand, don't benefit from higher prices, since peer production is based on *effort sharing*, not on profits. If some goods are distributed via *upward auctioning* due to insufficient supply, the only effect is that all the other goods distributed in the same pool become slightly cheaper, since the overall production effort is now distributed in a different way—the producers themselves won't benefit any more than everybody else participating in the pool.

Producers won't benefit from underproduction, but it does not really hurt them either. Therefore, prosumer associations might be less successful at avoiding underproduction than at avoiding overproduction. Unless you do it yourself, there is certainly no guarantee that anybody will start to produce a certain good, just because you would like to have it (and consider it worth the effort).

Still, the coordination in prosumer associations will help against underproduction too: in many cases, the people active in a project will like to expand their production, if they can be reasonably sure that their additional effort won't be wasted. One reason for this is that people who spend only part of their effort in a project might like to spend more or all of their production activities there if they enjoy the tasks they are doing within the project more than the tasks they are doing outside. Another is the psychological satisfaction of knowing that you do something that is useful to others, which is more obviously the case when you cater for needs that so far have not or not sufficiently been addressed.

Moreover, many producers will *also* be consumers ("prosumers") and as such they *will* be affected if underproduction leads to upward auctioning and hence higher prices of the goods they produce and consume. (Of course, they might also decide to produce just for themselves instead of taking part in a distribution pool, but such a decision would have other disadvantages: they would still have to contribute in other ways to a distribution pool to get access to goods produced by others; and production for a smaller group of people would probably be less efficient, leading to a similar rise in required effort as the upward auctioning.)

Note that such adjustment of supply to demand won't involve much planning overhead—much of it will occur spontaneously, by the individual decisions of projects that want to avoid wasting effort, and by the choices of people and projects looking for suitable new tasks to pick up. Still, some communications and agreements in prosumer associations will help people to reduce their risk of mistakes, and therefore will take place.

5.4.2. Optimizing Production

Another important effect of horizontal coordination can be the *optimization of production techniques.* By sharing their knowledge and experiences, including new techniques and inventions, projects can help each other to produce the same goods with less effort than before, or to produce goods that are better (from the point of view of the consumer) as before with the same effort. This would benefit those producers that are currently producing less efficient than others, but primarily it would benefit consumers, since it reduces the average effort they have to spend to get the goods they like.

Why should projects share their knowledge and insight with others? There are cases where the answer is clear: projects that are mainly producing for their own contributors (producers = consumers), or projects that are active for different local meta-projects, will clearly benefit by learning from the experiences of others, while they won't suffer a disadvantage by sharing their own experiences. However, if several projects are producing similar goods within the same distribution pool, addressing the same set of potential consumers, they have an incentive for secrecy: all else being equal, consumers will usually prefer the goods that take them less effort to get, so by producing more efficiently a project can extend its own production at the cost of the other projects.

Yet, this incentive for secrecy is far less strong than in a market economy, where increasing your market share is often a good way of increasing your profit rate. In peer production, there is no such effect. Since peer production is based on effort sharing, the result of attracting more consumers is merely that your project can contribute additional effort into a pool (the current project members can either work longer or accept additional members into the project). For the project members, this is not a large benefit: a mere increase in the number of members will hardly make participation in a project more pleasant than before. A member might prefer if she personally can contribute the effort required to get the goods she likes to have in the context of a single project instead of spreading it over several ones, but, except for very small projects, this should be possible in any case.

Hence, project members have little reason to prefer secrecy. On the other hand, they have various reasons to avoid secrecy:

1. Sharing will be good for your *reputation* (and also psychologically rewarding in itself), while secrecy will be bad. From the viewpoint of consumers, it is clearly advantageous if the projects producing the goods they want share their knowledge to optimize their production efforts. If you don't, you are clearly "doing the wrong thing" (cf. Sec. 2.3), and your potential consumers will not like it. They might well react by "shunning" your products (instead choosing those of projects that "share nicely"), either with the express purpose of "teaching you a lesson" or just instinctively.
   But your loss of reputation might not just drive consumers away, it will also make your project less attractive for potential *contributors* (whose own reputation depends in part on the projects they are in). This would cause the weight of tasks you distribute via task auctioning to go up (cf. Sec. 4.3.3), so your production effort (as measured in weighted hours) will actually *increase,* counteracting your attempt to keep it low.
2. In the long run, many cooperating projects will generally be more successful than a single non-cooperating one. If you refuse to share with others, they will probably respond by refusing to share with you, making it much

harder for to you keep up with whatever new inventions and insights *they* come up with.

3. Innovation will tend to spread anyway: attempts of keeping your innovations and optimizations secret will hardly be successful for very long. Sooner or later, others will find out what you did, either by reverse engineering your products or from people who have left your project or don't feel bound by your desire for secrecy. In capitalism, there are often laws that prohibit or restrict such "wild" innovation spreading, but in a peer economy people will hardly adopt or enact such laws, since in the context of peer production they don't fulfill any useful purpose.

We suppose that these incentives to prefer sharing over secrecy will typically prove to be stronger than the incentive for secrecy. More importantly, they will tend to make those who share more successful than those who don't. If this doesn't convince the latter to change their ways, they might well find themselves being left behind and becoming marginal.

5.4.3. Defining Standards and Guidelines

Another activity that prosumer associations might choose to handle is the definition of *standards* that improve interoperability between products, components, and accessories produced by different projects, thus facilitating future repairs and replacements, or that ensure that products are accessible to all kinds of people. Consumers will usually prefer projects who adhere to such standards (provided they are reasonable) so they won't become dependent on a single project for future upgrades or repairs of the things they are using. Projects following standards will thus generally be more successful. Projects planning to do so will have good reason to partake in the shaping of standards so they can influence the outcome and won't be surprised by it.

In addition to standards characterizing properties of the produced goods, prosumer associations might also publish guidelines on *how to* produce them. Guidelines might describe recommended practices and specify which activities and practices are considered unacceptable (e.g., because they are considered dangerous for the participants or for other people, harmful to the environment, or discriminating against specific groups of people).

Such guidelines might be less relevant for consumers, but they will influence the decisions of potential contributors. Provided the guidelines are reasonable, violating them will either mean that the working conditions of contributors become less agreeable or less safe or that their reputation is put at risk (your reputation will suffer if you are known to be in a project that "does the wrong thing," say by endangering the environment). Additionally, a prosumer association might decide to make adherence to standards and guidelines a precondition for full participation in the association.

Horizontal cooperation between projects active in the same sector of production will hardly be limited to the three forms we have discussed. Some other forms of such cooperation will be mentioned later throughout the text.

Also, there is no strict reason for these different forms of horizontal cooperation to be handled by a *single* association instead of by different institutions for different tasks (for example, standardization might be handled by a separate organization). We just use the umbrella term *prosumer associations* to refer to any such institutions that projects might set up to handle horizontal coordination tasks, regardless of the exact form they take.

5.5. Resource Allocation

Peer projects and local associations will often need natural resources for producing what they want. How to manage and allocate such resources?

5.5.1. Demand and Availability

Resource allocation only becomes a problem when the *demand* surpasses the *availability*—as long as there is enough of a resource available for everybody who wants to use it, there is no problem. *Demand* is established automatically by the summed decisions of all people and projects about what they want to consume or produce and which resources they need to do so.

Availability, however, is trickier to determine—if the whole amount of a non-renewable resource were considered to be available right now, it might soon be all used up, leaving nothing available for future generations. And for renewable resources, there often is a difference between *using them* and *using them up*. Land can potentially be used forever for purposes such as agriculture or farming, when used in a sensible way; but when used irresponsibly, the soil might be destroyed and the land will cease to be available, at least for some time.

Determining availability thus requires some decisions. Regarding non-renewable resources it must be decided how long they should last, i.e., which amount of them can be made available each year. Regarding renewable resources it must be decided whether they are available for *using up* (which is probably not a good idea, but might be necessary in some cases) or just for *using*. A third, and general, decision is which resources not to consider available for production at all, but to retain as they are (say if they are sacred places according to local tradition) or to use for other purposes (say as a wild forest or as a public park).

5.5.2. Local Management and Pooled Usage

Any specific resource is bound to the location where it occurs. Thus it makes sense to assume that the respective local associations (cf. Sec. 5.3) will have a say in making these decisions regarding availability. Note, however, that this does not mean that the local associations will *own* the resources—ownership, whether by communities or other institutions or by private persons, requires a *market* where you can buy resources that you need but don't own, and sell resources that you own but don't need. This is the same problem we discussed for housing (Sec. 4.4.2.5): ownership of resources would mean that this aspect of the economy falls outside the realm of peer production, and a complementary market economy is needed to handle it. The alternative, as in the case of housing, consists in considering resources to be part of the *commons*. They can be *managed* by the local associations they are in, but they are not *owned* by anybody.

Management of resources implies decisions about which resources to consider *available* (as discussed above) and how to share them. The problem of sharing resources is similar to the problem of sharing those results of a project that cannot be freely copied (cf. Sec. 4.4.2), which suggests that at least some of the possible solutions should also be similar.

Indeed, when the availability is higher than the demand, sharing is trivial: everybody can get what they want, which is essentially a *flat rate* model. If there is more demand than can be satisfied, *preference weighting*, i.e., the auctioning of available resources, is probably the most suitable model. *Flat allocation* would not make much sense since generally people would either get more of a resource than they can use or less than they need and nobody would be happy; accounting based on *production effort* isn't possible since natural resources are not produced by human labor.

But among whom are the available resources to be shared? If resources are considered as *commons*, it is clear that they do not belong to any specific group of people: ideally, they are shared among everybody, among mankind.

Above we had first discussed how the members of a single project can distribute their results among themselves (Sec. 4.4.2), but later observed that the participants of various projects will benefit if they join all their task and result allocation systems into a single system instead of using separate ones (the *distribution pool* model proposed in Sec. 5.2). The same argument applies for resources as well: the members of various local communities and regions will benefit if they *pool* their available resources, using the shared allocation system of an existing *distribution pool* to distribute the available resources of all participating local associations among all their inhabitants.

Thus, resources will be allocated through the chosen distribution pool in addition to tasks and products—though not everyone, but only inhabitants of the pooling local associations will be eligible to get these resources. If the availability of a resource is insufficient to satisfy the demands of all interested inhabitants on a flat-rate basis (i.e., for free), it will be auctioned among them: the resource will be assigned to the people willing to contribute most weighted labor to the pool in order to get it.

In this way, the resources of all participating local associations are available to all their inhabitants (and the projects they take part in), and the price (in weighted labor, as determined by the auctioning system) of a resource that cannot be shared on a flat-rate basis will be the same for all. If a project acquires resources that are not available for free (flat rate), it can add the weighted labor necessary to get them to the tasks the project members need to handle, so this additional labor will be distributed among them in the usual way.

5.5.3. Distributing Resources Through a Distribution Pool

A sufficiently large distribution pool avoids the problem that, without recurring to a market, resources that only occur in certain areas would not be available to the inhabitants of other areas at all, and resources that are rare in any given area would draw very high prices due to over-demand. Even communities and regions where natural resources of some kind are plentiful will generally benefit from participation in a distribution pool, since any local association is unlikely to have enough of *all* the resources its members need. Moreover, once resource distribution through distribution pools becomes usual, local associations will become *expected* to share them. Local associations that share their resources will hardly be willing to cooperate with others that don't. Therefore, local associations that try to treat resources as their property instead of as commons will find themselves not only without access to resources that do not occur in their area, but also without the cooperation partners they need to accomplish large-scale efforts.

We stated above (Sec. 5.2) that the emergence of a single global distribution pool instead of various smaller ones would be the best scenario. This is even more relevant for the distribution of resources than for the distribution of tasks and products, since only resource access through the same pool will ensure that everyone has fair access to any resources without being put at an advantage or disadvantage by the area they happen to live in. In fact, it is quite likely that such a single huge pool will emerge, since the members of peer projects and local associations will tend to join the largest pool which gives them the most variety of tasks, products, and resources to choose from.

Remember that resources are considered as *commons*, not as the property of the local associations where they occur. They are just made available as additional goods to be distributed in a pool. A high price paid for a resource won't go back to the association of origin; it just means that all the other available goods become slightly cheaper. This follows from the fact that resources are treated just like other goods that are distributed through the pool: if a project successfully distributes one of its products through the pool, the *effort* (in weighted labor) required to produce it will be recognized as a contribution to the pool. But natural resources are not produced, they just exist, so the production effort to be recognized is zero.

Of course, the *usage* of resources often involves effort, but any efforts necessary for getting and utilizing resources will be up to those who use them—what is pooled is only the *right* to use a resource. In practice, there will often be specialized projects for obtaining and transporting resources, and most acquirers of resources will probably entrust such tasks to one of them (recognizing their effort in the usual way) instead of handling the resources directly.

Since resources are commons, the *right to use* a resource probably won't include the *right to sell* it. People and projects who get resources on a flat-rate or auctioning basis will be able to use them for their own activities, but they will hardly be allowed to sell them or to use them for the production of goods that are meant to be sold; otherwise, especially flat-rate access would quickly break down. Of course, such a provision to *keep the commons common* (i.e., not to turn them into property), which resembles the *copyleft* clause of the GNU General Public License (cf. Sec. 4.4.1), will only be relevant as long as a peer production–based economy and a market-based economy co-exist.

If resources are considered as commons that are distributed through a distribution pool, decisions regarding resource availability become quite sensitive, because they shape the extent of the commons. This is one aspect of decision making in a peer economy—an issue to which we will turn next.

5.6. Decision Making

Studies such as Schweik and English (2007) show that current peer projects tend to favor institutions and processes for decision making and conflict resolution that are lean and unobtrusive. And we had already stated (in Sec. 2.2) that peer production lacks the elements of coercion that are typical for other systems of production. We may expect that future peer institutions and processes will be similarly lean and non-coercive.

There are mainly two purposes which peer institutions have to fulfill: they need to organize shared production and they need to deal with conflicts between members if the people concerned fail to resolve them by themselves. Current institutions (such as states) often pursue additional goals, trying to regulate people's lives far beyond what is necessary for the purposes of organizing production and resolving conflicts. As far as we can see, such tendencies of controlling people's lives are absent from current peer projects, and we see no reasons why they should re-appear in the future.

5.6.1. Aspects of Decision Making

In the context of peer production, two aspects of decision making can be observed: the *meritocratic* aspect and the *democratic* aspect.

In current peer projects, it is often a single person or a small number of persons that have ultimate decision-making power. In many free software projects (especially in smaller ones) there is a single *maintainer* (lead developer) who decides which contributions to accept and which features to add and who is responsible for resolving any disputed issues regarding the architecture and design of the software. In larger projects, there are often some domain specialists responsible for maintaining and managing certain components or aspects of the system (sub-maintainers); sometimes a *core team* of several persons jointly fills the maintainer role. People tend to get such positions based on their initiative (e.g., as project founder) or because of their (perceived) capabilities and expertise, hence free software projects are often described as *meritocratic* (cf. Schweik and English, 2007; Lehmann, 2004).

The individuals trusted with such roles are generally expected to "do the right thing" instead of just making arbitrary decisions according to their personal preferences. The (perceived) ability to "do the right thing," to decide in the way that makes most sense from a technological or social point of view and that is likely to be best for the project, has a strong positive influence on people's *reputation* and on their chances of being accepted for and successful in such roles (cf. Sec. 2.3).

In current peer projects, the *democratic* aspect mainly comes in two forms:

- People "vote with their feet," supporting the projects they like, and leaving or forking a project if they are unhappy about the way in which it evolves.
- Project participants generally strive for *consensus* or, at least, *rough consensus,* resorting to maintainer decisions only in those rare cases where rough consensus fails to emerge.

The concept of *rough consensus* has first become popular through its usage in the Internet Engineering Task Force (IETF), which explains it as follows:

> Working groups make decisions through a "rough consensus" process. IETF consensus does not require that all participants agree although this is, of course, preferred. In general, the dominant view of the working group shall prevail. (However, it must be noted that "dominance" is not to be determined on the basis of volume or persistence, but rather a more general sense of agreement.) (IETF, 1998, Sec. 3.3)

Majority voting is seldom used in current peer projects. The open character of many projects makes it hard to clearly and fairly determine who is and who isn't sufficiently involved to be eligible to vote. Also, most current projects communicate primarily over the Internet, which would make it very hard to prevent people from assuming additional identities (called "sock puppets" in the Wikipedia community) and voting several times. A further reason for majority votes being rare is the stability of projects: a project deciding on a controversial issue with a narrow majority would risk losing a large part of its participants, since those unhappy about the decision can always leave the project, possibly *forking* it by founding their own alternative project.

The "enforcement" of rules and decisions is often based on *technical means* (somebody without write access to the code repository cannot damage the source code of a project) as well as on *trust;* most projects manage to do quite well without formal control and sanction mechanisms. If people accidentally or (quite seldom) intentionally violate the rules, they are usually just told that they did wrong and admonished not to do so again; mostly this happens in a friendly fashion, but more aggressive and scolding "flames" occur as well, especially in more serious cases (cf. Schweik and English, 2007). Due to the important role of *reputation,* trying to give somebody negative reputation by "flaming and shunning" them tends to be a powerful way of sanctioning people if less aggressive ways prove ineffectual. If all else fails, *boycott* and *exclusion* remain as the toughest sanctioning mechanisms: the concerned person might be removed from communication channels (such as mailing lists), she will lose her rights of making contributions to the project (losing repository write access if she had any), and she will generally be boycotted and ignored (cf. Lehmann, 2004).

5.6.2. Decision Making in Peer Projects

We suppose that future peer projects will pursue similar ways of decision making as the current ones, striving for *rough consensus* and trusting *maintainers* and other responsible experts to "do the right thing," especially in regard to technical issues.

One difference to the current situation is that we would not be surprised if projects that *require* contributions will rely more heavily on democratic decisions, including majority voting (at least as fallback mechanism) than current projects, which are generally based on voluntarism (cf. Sec. 4.2). In such projects, the problem of deciding who is eligible to vote and to prevent duplicate votes becomes void since voting rights can be tied to contributions; and when people have to make a certain amount of contributions, it seems reasonable to assume that they will want to have more say in regard to the activities of the projects.

However, the concern that narrow majority votes would endanger the stability of projects still applies. Thus, even projects that require contributions will probably strive for rough consensus whenever possible, falling back to majority voting only as a last resort when consensus cannot be reached.

Another way of ensuring the influence of contributors while keeping the meritocratic character of peer projects would be to assign *revocable positions* for maintainers, sub-maintainers and other special roles. This would mean that the chosen persons can make the decisions they deem appropriate; but when the project members are dissatisfied with the decisions of a specialist, they can revoke her (possibly canceling her last decisions) and appoint a new person for her role.

5.6.3. Decision Making in Local Associations

5.6.3.1. Organization of Local Meta-Projects

Since the primary purpose of local associations in a peer economy is the providing of infrastructure and public services (cf. Sec. 5.3), a major part of local decision making will regard the coordination of these activities in local meta-projects. We may expect that their ways of decision making will be comparable to those of regular peer projects, comprising both meritocratic and democratic aspects.

We would not be surprised if people will prefer the *democratic* mode for decisions regarding *which* kinds of infrastructure and public services to organize and how to make them available (cf. Sec. 5.3.1); but the *meritocratic* mode for decisions about *how* these activities are organized, trusting detail decisions to the projects and persons actually handling a specific task. This would give all the inhabitants of a local association a say in regard to which infrastructures and services they will get, while leaving the details of providing these services to the experts doing the actual work.

However, this trust will probably not be unconditional—more likely, local associations will reserve some rights of *democratic override* for themselves, allowing their members to question and if necessary cancel any detail decisions they are unhappy about (possibly requiring a supermajority of, for example, 60% for such override decisions). The people and projects doing the actual work will then have to decide whether they can go along with the democratic decision; if not, the local association will no longer recognize their activities as contributions to the meta-project. In that case they would have to look for other tasks to do for the local association, while the association would need to find other people taking over their work.

While we stated above that peer projects tend to aim for *rough consensus* when making democratic decisions, we doubt that this will be the preferred mode for deciding which infrastructures and public services to provide—there is no good reason not to organize any specific service just because 5% or 10% of the people don't think it necessary. Instead, simple majority voting or even quorum voting (a task will be organized if a quorum of, say, at least 25% of all voters deem it useful) makes more sense for such decisions. It also seems reasonable to accept stakeholder-specific decisions regarding the concerns of specific groups of people—for example, questions regarding education and child care mainly concern children and their parents, so it seems reasonable to consider a majority or quorum of *their* votes to be sufficient for decisions regarding these questions.

5.6.3.2. Resource Availability

Another kind of decisions the people living in an area will have to make concern the *availability* of resources occurring in their area (cf. Sec. 5.5). If resources are pooled as *commons,* such decisions regarding availability become quite sensitive. They affect not just the specific local association where a resource occurs, but also all the *other* local associations pooling their resources. If all local association were to make their decisions independently from each other and one of them decides to keep back many of its resources, the other ones might get the impression that it wants to benefit from their resources but is not willing to give back. The likely result is that other local associations would react by sharing less of their own resources, which might well cause the whole resource pooling system to break down.

The local associations participating in a pool thus need to find a way of conciliating the concerns of the people living in a specific area with the concerns of all the other people pooling their resources. One way of doing this it to set up a *bottom-up* mechanism for making availability decisions.

We already pointed out that there will be several levels of local associations (cf. Sec. 5.3.2). Bottom-up decisions could start at a comparatively localized level, say the level of *local communities.* Each local community makes proposals regarding the availability of resources occurring in its area and passes these proposals to the next-highest level *(regions).* Each region merges the proposals from the local communities into an integrated proposal which is passed to the next *(superregional)* level; and so on (after the superregional, there may be a *global* level, if various superregions share their resources in the same pool).

The decisions of each larger local association would be made by a board of delegates from the smaller associations constituting it; the board would make its proposal based on—but not strictly bound by—the proposals of the smaller associations (cf. Sec. 7.1.2 for more on the organization of such decision-making structures). In this way, nobody needs to fear that decisions regarding locally available resources are made by some remote agency which has little clue about the local situation; but neither can some of the participating local associations arbitrarily withhold resources while benefiting from those of others.

5.6.4. Decision Making in Prosumer Associations

Since prosumer associations (Sec. 5.4) are just "meta-projects" that don't produce or organize anything on their own, there won't be that many day-to-day decisions to be made. Most decisions will concern the coordination of production to better adjust supply to demand (cf. Sec. 5.4.1) and the definition of standards and guidelines (cf. Sec. 5.4.3). The third activity of prosumer associations we had discussed—the sharing of experiences and knowledge to optimize production (cf. Sec. 5.4.2)—will mainly be informal without requiring decisions.

We assume that these decisions will typically require a *rough consensus* or at least a strong majority among the involved projects. Rough consensus is already the typical mode of decision making in standards organization such as the IETF (quoted above) or the World Wide Web Consortium (W3C). And since prosumer associations cannot *force* projects to produce or not to produce something, (rough) consensus among the concerned projects is the only realistic option to ensure that the decisions of the association on how to handle supply are implemented as agreed.

This does not necessarily mean that the horizontal coordination between projects in the same sector would come to a halt if there are some projects that refuse to become part of a rough consensus. In such cases it is always possible for the remaining projects to make agreements (how to adjust supply or which standards and guidelines to follow) among themselves. Such a limited consensus would be less satisfactory than a consensus among all relevant projects, but it would still offer practical advantages for the participating projects (for supply coordination, they can decide to share the risk of overproduction among themselves, thus mitigating the individual risk of any project; consumers and contributors will tend to prefer projects adhering to prevalent standards and responsible guidelines over those that don't). The possible effects on *reputation* are another factor promoting consensus building: projects that block decisions will have to be careful to give good reasons for their behavior, otherwise they risk being perceived as irresponsible which wouldn't help their reputation.

How to organize decision making in practice? One way of doing so would be to set up a *coordination board* comprising one delegate for each participating project. If a prosumer association becomes too large for delegates of all projects to be present in a single board, they could introduce an interim level by grouping the participating projects by location and/or by more specialized activity domains, and establish a specific coordination board for each group of projects. Each of these specific coordination boards would then choose a delegate to send to the main coordination board; domain-specific coordination boards could also directly decide on any agreements, standards, and guidelines concerning their specific domain of activity.

6. Comparison with Other Modes of Production

We now know enough about how an economy based on peer production might work to be able to compare it with alternative modes of production.

6.1. Differences from a Market Economy

Today, the globally dominant economy is clearly the *market-based* mode of production, also known as *capitalism.* Due to the important role of auctioning, which is also employed in market-based production, the proposed model might appear to be similar to the market. Indeed, the usage of auctioning has effects that are similar to some effects of the market, since both remove the need for hierarchical planning and/or extensive discussions that would otherwise be necessary to distribute tasks, products, and resources. Nevertheless, the differences are striking.

6.1.1. No More Indirection

The fundamental difference—the one difference that causes all the others—is that the peer economy *directly* achieves the goal which the market achieves only *indirectly* (if at all): fulfilling people's *needs and desires,* making it possible for them to get what they want to have and to live the way they want to live. In the peer economy, you cooperate with others to get the goods you like to have, while in the market economy you produce one thing to get money which *then* allows you to get other things.

Peer production cuts out the middle layer—the need to sell so you can buy. This change goes very deep, since in capitalism the apparently harmless middle layer (the need to make money) takes over and becomes the primary goal of production, shifting the original goal (fulfilling people's needs and desires) into the background.

6.1.2. No Need to Sell—No Unemployment

In the market, you need money to get the goods you like to buy. If you don't have enough money, you need to sell something, and if you don't have anything else, you need to sell your own labor capacity. But if nobody wants your labor, you are out of luck. You are *unemployed* and will generally remain poor and unable to get most of the things you would like to have.

In peer production there is no need to sell, neither your labor capacity nor anything else. You will often be expected to invest some labor to get the things you like to have, but this is only to contribute your share to the overall effort. If there is nothing left to do, there is no reason to work, hence the term "unemployment" does not even make sense in the context of a peer economy.

Whether and how much you work will depend only on the effort necessary to get the goods you like to have. There is no reason to work more and, in effect, it won't even be possible to make more contributions that will be recognized as such, because, quite simple, there is "nothing left to do."

6.1.3. Demand-driven Instead of Profit-driven Production

This is because peer production is entirely *demand-driven*, while market production is *profit-driven*.

In peer production, things are produced and services are organized if there are people who want to have them and who are willing to jointly spend the amount of labor that is necessary to get them. In the market, conversely, prior demand is neither a sufficient nor a necessary condition for production. If a company feels it can make a profit from selling a line of products, it might work very hard on instilling demand in potential customers; in fact, a good part of the effort of market production goes into suggesting to people that they do have demand for a specific product, whether they knew it or not.

On the other hand, demand, no matter how urgent, is not enough to get a good produced. The market will not satisfy demand if potential producers cannot make a profit from selling to those who have the demand, or if they can make a higher profit by producing something else. If you are poor, your demands don't count, unless they can be satisfied very cheaply.

In peer production, no other preconditions are required apart from the willingness to contribute your share to the overall effort. It does not matter whether you are poor or rich. In fact, these concepts do not even exist: some people will have more things, others will have less, depending on their wishes and preferences, but this does not influence their chances of fulfilling any future needs.

In capitalism, the necessity to make profit does not only influence which goods are produced, but also how they are produced. Firms will be more successful if they keep not only their current, but also their future profits in mind. Thus the tendency of trying to "lock in" customers to prevent them from switching over to the competition, and the tendency to build products in such a way that they need expensive accessories and expensive repairs or replacements if and when they break down. They have no incentive to increase the longevity of their products beyond that of the competition, since doing so would only cut into their profits. And since they often benefit from selling resources and refills their products require, the have little incentive to decrease resource usage.

In peer production, it would be silly to increase the effort necessary for using, repairing, or replacing the things you produce. Since the necessary effort is shared among all, it would only mean that you have more to do.

In peer production, there is no necessity to make profit that influences which goods are produced and how they are produced. Instead, it is people's preferences and priorities that decide how they live and which goods (including services) they produce. Areas such as health care and elder care will no longer be subjected to profitability concerns, and neither will anything else.

6.1.4. Competition Gets a Different Face

None of this is meant to imply that market players are in any way immoral or bad. They are not. It's simply that they do not have any other choice, if they want to survive as market players.

They *cannot* choose to cut profits out of other considerations, unless all their competitors do the same (which they will hardly do, unless forced by law). They *have* to reduce the cost of production as far as possible, or else the customers will tend to flock to competitors who are able to produce and hence sell cheaper. And they *have* to keep their level of profits similar to those of competing companies and of other sectors, or the capital they need to keep or extend their market share will tend to flow elsewhere (the latter point might be irrelevant for small privately owned companies that do not need external capital, but these usually find it hard enough to survive next to far larger competitors anyway, so they have little or no space to behave better than the giants). The rules of market competition ensure that companies *must* think primarily of their profits—they cannot behave in any other way, or they will lose in the market.

Conversely, in the peer economy, competition gets a different face. For a project to be successful, it needs to attract sufficient contributors to reach its goals. As long as projects working on similar products both reach this goal, they have no need to out-compete each other. In so far as they compete, it will be more like a sporty challenge, each trying to show the others that you can do better than they. It will be more a game than a serious matter since the survival of the projects does not depend on it.

As for attracting contributors, efficiency will still be an important factor for success: a project that manages to produce equivalent goods with a lower amount of weighted labor will be more attractive for users since they have to contribute less to get what they like to have. But not all means of increasing efficiency that work in capitalism will work in a peer economy. Bad labor conditions or lax security standards, for example, will hardly be a successful way of attracting contributors. Actually, such efforts would backfire even from an efficiency standpoint: worse working conditions would make the respective tasks less popular for potential contributors, causing their weight in the task auctioning system to go up. So even if the amount of (unweighted) labor hours for producing an item in such a way would be lower, its cost as measured in *weighted* labor would probably be higher.

Other ways of increasing efficiency that are common in the market would hardly be successful in a peer economy due to the important role of *reputation* in peer production (cf. Sec. 2.3). Reputation depends on the perception of a person or project "doing the right thing," and projects damaging the environment or engaging in other harmful or dangerous behavior would hardly be perceived as "doing the right thing." Their reputation would dwindle, making it hard for them to attract contributors, whose own reputation would suffer if they were connected with such a project.

Similarly, keeping your business methods, knowledge, and software secret is a frequent strategy of keeping a competitive advantage in the market, but it would hardly work in peer production with its philosophy of commons and sharing. Violating this philosophy would hurt your reputation. Conversely, sharing your knowledge and your ideas is a certain way of increasing your reputation (provided they are good). In a market, it is a problem for companies if their new ideas or methods are copied by others, since it takes away their advantage in producing cheaper. In peer production, it is an advantage, since many people will remember where the new ideas came from, and your reputation will rise.

6.1.5. No Separation of Centers and Periphery

Market competition is a "game" that allows only a limited number of winners. This leads to a tendency of the production of specific goods to concentrate in the hands of a few corporations that have managed to out-compete the others (or to buy them—corporate mergers are an important ingredient of success strategies since smaller players often lack the capacity to compete with larger ones).

The establishment of such successful global players is hardly possible without high amounts of capital to invest. Thus these corporations tend to be headquartered in—or at least financed from—one of the centers of capitalist production (mainly North America, Western Europe, and parts of Asia). This does not necessarily mean that the actual production takes place in these centers—they are just where most of the profits go.

For the people outside these centers it is very hard to compete successfully, since they usually lack the necessary capital to do so. While it is not impossible to establish new centers (as the Asian example shows), there is no way in which *every* country or region could become a center. The existence of centers depends on the existence of the periphery just like the existence of winners depends on the existence of losers.

Peer production renders the separation of centers and periphery obsolete, since it doesn't require capital or other preconditions for successful participation and since peer projects don't compete in the same way as companies do. No matter where people live, as long as they find enough co-participants they can establish a successful project, without having to outcompete projects pursuing similar activities.

In peer production, people jointly produce for themselves, not for the market. People everywhere will be able to produce for themselves whatever they would like to have; and since peer production tends to treat knowledge and resources as commons that are to be shared, they will all have similar preconditions for doing so.

6.1.6. No Need to Reinvent the Wheel and Little Other Overhead

Due to the tendency of peer production to favor openness and sharing, innovations will spread much faster. They will also require far less efforts to spread. In the market, companies have to make huge efforts trying to duplicate innovations introduced by their competitors (and in such a way that they won't violate any patents or copyrights of them). Alternatively, they have to do without the innovations, meaning that they create products that won't be as good as they could be otherwise or whose production will take a higher effort than it would otherwise.

In either case, the tendency of the market to keep innovations secret or to treat them as property imposes a large amount of additional labor that is unnecessary in a peer economy. In peer production, there is no need to reinvent any wheels that have already been invented by others. Any innovations can immediately be adapted by whoever wants to use them; and any further improvements made by others can immediately flow back to the original innovator.

There are lots of other activities that are necessary or useful in the market context but won't be needed in a peer economy. Peer projects have little or no reason to instill demand for their products (cf. Sec. 6.1.3); they do not need to monitor the activities of "competing" projects as closely as companies do (since they aren't competing in the market sense); and the whole overhead of acquiring and retaining capital and keeping shareholders happy will be gone.

Even more significant is the overhead imposed by the market system outside of companies. Today, people spend innumerable hours trying to look for a job (especially those who cannot find one) or training for better jobs without getting them, and a huge bureaucracy is needed to deal with the jobless. There are whole industries for investing and lending money and for managing the profits accrued in the market. None of this is necessary in a peer economy.

Moreover, the control structures imposed by current society —laws, police, prisons, governments—are mainly needed to upkeep the private property regime that the market requires (to prevent people from selling or using things that are supposed to be owned by others) and to prevent people from acquiring money in ways that are considered socially unacceptable. A peer economy, where there is no need to earn money and where people can get whatever they want by contributing to a project of their choice, will only need much leaner versions of such structures, if at all (cf. Sec. 8.4 for a longer discussion on which laws and regulations might still be necessary).

Not only will peer production grant people an unprecedented amount of control over their own lives, it will also require much less work for doing so. Without the need for all the overhead activities imposed by the market and the private property regime, peer production can reach an efficiency the most ardent advocates of the market cannot even dream of.

6.1.7. The Peer Economy Works Around Scarcity, It Does Not Need It

Markets only work for goods that are *scarce,* i.e., for which the demand is higher than the available supply. Without scarcity, when the supply of a good surpasses the demand, the market price for the good will tend to tumble as each of the competing producers tries to extend or to preserve their market share. This will reduce the supply, since some of the producers will not be able to produce so efficiently that they can sell at the reduced price and still make a profit, or they will turn to other business areas that allow them to draw a higher profit from the invested capital. The price drop thus ensures that the supply of a good falls until it is sufficiently scarce for prices to stabilize again.

The resulting scarcity, however, follows from the decisions of producers, it is not absolute. Usually, each producer *could* easily increase the produced amount to fulfill additional demand, but they will not do so if it would hurt their profits. They will not sell at prices that would degrade their profit level—indeed, they *cannot,* or their competition is likely to get the better of them, as discussed above. Because of this, markets will hardly ever satisfy *all* demand, since not everyone will be able to afford the price level that is best for profits.

Also, goods can only be sold in the market if people have reason to *buy* them, and they won't buy goods that they can get in any other way that saves them the cost of buying. Therefore the sellers in a market will generally try to destroy or outlaw any alternatives that would allow people to access the goods they produce (or similar ones) without paying for them. Therefore companies whose business model is based on selling software, music, or movies require copyright laws to prevent people from just copying the items they are expected to pay for, making things scarce that otherwise wouldn't be (once they have been produced).

Of course, the argument for such scarcity laws is that without them, the items in question would not be produced at all, since they couldn't be produced with a profit. *Within the context of the market system,* this is often enough true (not always, since markets players are good at finding different business models if any specific one doesn't work). In the market, only things that can be produced with a profit will be produced at all, and only things that are scarce in some way or other can be produced with a profit. Markets thus not only require scarcity to remain stable, they also induce it in any good they touch.

Peer production, on the other hand, does not *need* scarcity at all. Instead, it treats scarcity as a problem to be dealt with. And without the tendency of the market to induce it, scarcity will probably not even be a very serious problem. Without the scarcity induced by the necessity to make profits, only two sources of scarcity remain: the limited availability of human labor, and the limited availability of natural resources.

Human labor, however, is not really scarce, as the existence of massive unemployment and underemployment in current economies shows. It will probably be even less scarce in a peer production–based economy due to the efficiency increases outlined above. Which goods are produced in a peer economy and which aren't does not depend on scarcity of human labor but on the *priorities* of people.

Peer projects may be unable to reach their goals because they fail to attract sufficient participants willing to make the necessary contributions, but this is not a matter of the scarcity of human labor—after all, the non-participants will hardly all work until they drop. Instead, it expresses the priorities of people: in such a case, most of them obviously prefer to spend their lives in other ways than by contributing to the project in question—even if they wouldn't mind having the products of the project, they apparently don't consider it worth the effort. Faced with a trade-off, they have made a decision. In peer production, what is and what isn't produced depends on the *choices* of people, not on scarcity.

The limited availability of natural resources will continue to be a problem in some cases, but with the resource allocation model proposed above (Sec. 5.5) it will merely be a factor that influences people's decisions. Since scarce resources are auctioned among those who want to use them, the effort required to produce a good that needs such a scarce resource will automatically increase, and this will affect people's decisions about whether or not they are really willing the make the necessary effort. Those who care most about the products for which they need the resources will be willing to spend the most effort to get them; and since effort is measured in weighted labor, everybody will be in the same position when deciding whether or not to make it. Whether or not scarce resources are involved, peer production is driven by people's decisions about where their priorities lie and how much they really care for any good.

6.2. Differences from a Planned Economy

Since planned economies have not been very popular since the collapse of the Soviet Union (or even before), there is probably little need for a detailed critique and comparison. The central difference between planned economies and a peer economy is, of course, that in a peer economy there is no need for hierarchical planning processes to decide which goods to produce and how to allocate goods and resources. Peer production avoids the whole bureaucratic overhead that is necessary for a planned economy. In fact, as we have seen above, the bureaucratic overhead that is needed for a peer economy is lower than the overhead of the market, which in turn is lower than the overhead of a planned economy.

More important than the overhead is the fact that people living in a peer economy are in full control over their lives, while in a planned economy they are not. In a peer economy, there are no institutions that decide which people should do which tasks and which resources they may use to do so. Instead, everybody can decide according to their own preferences—of course, the decisions of others will affect your own, by influencing the value of tasks and resources in the auctioning systems, but the ultimate decision is up to you.

Planned production chronically suffers from planning errors, where the production fails to satisfy all actual demand or where unneeded items are produced. While this might be considered a merely technical problem that could be addressed by improved processes, the deeper problem remains that a planned economy necessarily has to *judge and prioritize* the needs of the people living in it. A planned economy has to decide which of your needs are sufficiently important to be satisfied and which are not, but these are decision which cannot really be made by anybody else than by you (no matter whether such decisions are made by an elite of planners or entirely democratic).

In the market, needs are generally not judged (which is good), but your chances of satisfying them depend largely on the money you happen to have. In peer production, needs are not judged and they are prioritized only by the person who has them. You can satisfy any needs without needing anybody's permission and without needing money, as long as you are able and willing to make the necessary effort (which will very often make it necessary to convince other people to cooperate with you, since you would not be able to undertake the necessary labor all by yourself), and as long as your needs do not interfere with other people's lives in ways they are unwilling to accept (how to deal with such conflicts will be discussed in Sec. 7.2).

Planned economies also suffer from the problem that producers often have little incentive to care for the quality of their products. They usually don't produce for their use, but for others; and since products are produced and allocated as decided by a planning institution, the consumers have little choice but to take what they get. In market systems, producers also produce for others, but they must care for the quality of their products sufficiently to prevent consumers from turning to the competition. It is the fear of economic failure that ensures the quality of products—but only in so far as consumers are likely to notice, and only when there are competitors that feel that it would benefit their profit level to do better than you. Peer production goes further by abolishing the distinction between producers and consumers—people jointly produce for their own use, and thus have every incentive to make their products as good as they want them to be.

The dependency on bureaucratic decision making for resource access explains two further problems that have been observed in the Soviet bloc: the tendency to apply for more resources than you really need (for the quite likely case that you will only be granted a fraction of what you applied for); and the tendency to *hoard* resources that you don't currently need but might need in the future (since you don't know whether you would be granted them when you need them). With the proposed auctioning system for resources that cannot be made available to all, peer production will not have such problems.

Even modern variants of planned economies that claim to be highly democratic and participatory—such as the *Parecon* ("participatory economics") concept proposed by Michael Albert (2004)—would impose a tremendous planning overhead, and would interfere with people's lives to a high degree. (In Parecon, this interference comes largely in the form of "balanced job complexes," forcing people to do a variety of very different tasks instead of letting them decide according to their strengths and preferences.)

Oscar Wilde is supposed to have said that "the trouble with socialism is that it takes too many evenings," which characterizes the planning and decision-making overhead of planned economies quite well. Capitalism, on the other hand, takes too many days which people have to spend doing work (or looking for work) for which they often don't specifically care, but which they have to do in order to earn the money they need. The peer economy gives the control over both your evenings and your days back to you.

7. Aspects of Life in a Peer Economy

Peer projects and local associations are self-organizing—the participating people will figure out for themselves how to arrange their lives. Still, since we are interested to learn more about how life in a peer economy might be like, we will try to make some educated guesses about their decisions.

7.1. Forms of Democratic Decision Making in Local Associations

In Section 5.6.3 we discussed which modes the inhabitants of local associations will prefer for decisions of local concern. We supposed that they would prefer the democratic mode for cardinal decisions such as which kinds of public services and infrastructure to organize, while generally trusting details of how to do so to the projects and people doing the actual work. Democracy, however, comes in different shapes, and which of them is most suitable depends on various factors such as the number of people involved. Which modes of democratic decision making can we expect to be employed in the organization of local associations?

7.1.1. Decision Making in Local Communities and Neighborhoods

Local communities with about 100,000 to 500,000 members (cf. Sec. 5.3.2.1) should still be sufficiently small to rely on *direct democracy* where all the people are eligible to make proposals (for tasks to organize etc.) and to vote on proposals. Both *agenda setting* (making proposals) and *voting* can be supported quite efficiently by software-based solutions.

There is, of course, another essential step between these two steps: *discussing* the proposals made. This step is more tricky, since local communities will generally be too large for face-to-face meetings of *all* the people interested in discussing; and software-based discussion channels (such as mailing lists or discussion boards) are a good complement for face-to-face discussions, but hardly a fully adequate substitute.

Electronic discussion forums at the communal level could, however, be conveniently complemented with a *two-level* process for face-to-face discussions, by relying on the *neighborhoods* within a community for the first level. With about five hundred to a few thousand inhabitants (cf. Sec. 5.3.2.3), neighborhoods are small enough to allow everyone who cares to participate in face-to-face discussions; the participants of such neighborhood discussions could then send delegates to discussions at the community level for voicing opinions and concerns expressed during a neighborhood meeting. There would be about one hundred to a few hundred neighborhoods in a community, making such delegate discussions quite feasible in size.

Together with online discussions at the community level, such a two-level discussion process should allow everyone interested to get a clear picture of any decisions to make. Anyway, we suppose that *communal meta-projects* will tend to run quite smoothly without the need for much intervention; so there probably won't be that many decisions to make, once an initial set of infrastructures and services to provide has been agreed on and some basic decisions regarding the joining of a *distribution pool* and the availability of resources have been made.

Similarly, we suppose that *neighborhoods* will not require many formal decisions, since they are mainly coordination points for *ad hoc* cooperation. As stated above, neighborhoods are sufficiently small to allow face-to-face meetings, so relying on direct democracy for what democratic decisions are still to be made in this context shouldn't be a problem.

7.1.2. Decision Making at the Regional Level and Beyond

Which modes of democratic decision making can we expect to be employed for local decisions beyond the community level, regarding the organization of *regional meta-projects* and any superregional cooperation?

As stated above (Sec. 5.3.2.2), *regions* might comprise about 30 to 50 local communities with about 3 to 15 million inhabitants. While *direct democracy* could still be an option for such sizes, the problem of discussions becomes even harder. Instead, regions might prefer to organize themselves as networks of communities in a similar way to prosumer associations (cf. Sec. 5.6.4), by setting up a *regional coordination board* comprising one delegate for each participating community. Thus it would be this coordination board of about 30 to 50 delegates that makes the actual decisions regarding the organization of the respective *regional meta-project* and related issues; the inhabitants of each community would elect a delegate for this board. Since the task of delegates would not be to decide arbitrarily, but to speak for their community, we can expect that such delegate positions would be *revocable* (cf. Sec. 5.6.2) and that delegates would be bound by any specific decisions of their community.

This form of organization scales well to further levels of cooperation. If regions decide to cooperate at the superregional level, each of the participating *regional coordination boards* could choose a delegate (any person they deem fit, not necessarily a board member) to send to a *superregional coordination board* which decides on the organization of superregional activities. And for those tasks that they decide to handle on the global level, superregions can appoint a *global coordination board* in the same way. Similar to regional delegates, these superregional and global delegates would probably be bound by any decisions of the board that sent them.

7.1.3. Who Will Be Eligible to Take Part in Decisions?

The evolution of democracy shows a clear tendency to include more and more people in the democratic process. In early democracies such as ancient Greece, only a small minority of people was eligible to take part in decisions (typically males of "good origin" and with their own household). Since then, the criteria for inclusion have gradually expanded. In current democracies, almost everybody is eligible to participate, with two notable exceptions: children and teens as well as "foreigners."

We suppose that, in the context of a peer economy, the expansion of the inclusion process will continue and these remaining exclusions will sooner or later fall. This is especially relevant regarding the status of "foreigners": most likely, everybody who is living in a local association for more then just a few weeks (or maybe months) will be expected to contribute their share to the local meta-projects; but for everybody who is expected to contribute, it is essential that they also have a right to take part in decisions. Otherwise they would be required to work for goals which they did not choose and cannot influence, which would be a kind of forced labor and hardly fits the pattern of non-coercive cooperation that is characteristic for peer production.

Children, on the other hand, probably won't be expected to contribute (cf. Sec. 8.1.1). This could be brought forward as an argument to exclude them from the decision making process. However, following this argument, old and ill people would have to be excluded as well, which is not the case today and does not sound like a good idea.

The alternative is to allow *everybody* living in a local association to take part in the democratic process if and when they want to do so, no matter their age or origin—this also fits better with the tendency of peer production to move from status to reputation (cf. Sec. 2.3) which renders outward characteristics such as age less important. Obviously, babies won't be able to take part in decisions, and five-year-olds will generally have other things on their minds; but we can see no plausible reason why children and teens should be excluded if and when they *want* to participate.

7.2. Stakeholder Involvement and Conflict Resolution

Peer projects, local associations, and prosumer associations will have decision making structures (cf. Sec. 5.6) that can deal with any conflicts concerning the organization of the project or association. However, not all conflicts occur in such a context. What if there are conflicts between different projects or between a project and a local association; what about conflicts between people that are unrelated to organizational issues?

It is important to realize that real conflicts about any action can only occur between *stakeholders*, i.e., between people that would both be affected by the action, at least potentially. If you are not a stakeholder, you might be unhappy about other people's actions, but they are no real concern for you. There is (for example) no reason for the Pope to intervene in other people's sex lives, unless they want to have sex with him. Any person can give *recommendations* to other people about how they should live their lives, but whether or not they listen is entirely up to them.

Stakeholders, on the other hand, clearly can expect to be involved in any decisions that concern them. It would hardly be fair if any person or institution could make decisions that seriously affect other people's lives (if only potentially, e.g., in case of accidents) without their having a say in this matter. In any such cases, the principle of consensus, or that least rough consensus, seems reasonable; meaning that the stakeholders, or at least most of them, have to reach an agreement for any decision to be put into action.

A society can set up institutions to help ensuring that people know about activities that might affect them in a non-trivial way and that others cannot decide upon such activities behind their back *(stakeholder involvement)* and to arbitrate if agreement fails to emerge *(conflict resolution).* This might be a suitable task for the various levels of local associations discussed above (Sec. 5.3.2), since effects are often limited to specific areas. This would result in five levels:

1. The *neighborhood level,* comprising about five hundred to a few thousand people.
2. The *communal level,* comprising about 100,000 to 500,000 people (in one hundred to several hundred *neighborhoods*).
3. The *regional level,* comprising about 3 to 15 million people (in about 30 to 50 *local communities*).
4. The *superregional level,* comprising about 150 to 500 million people (in about 30 to 50 *regions*).
5. And the *global level,* comprising everybody on Earth (in a dozen or a few dozen *superregions*).

To ensure that they are informed about decisions that concern them, people at each level could choose a delegate to send to an *information board* at the next highest level. Thus there would be four levels of information boards, from the communal level (comprising delegates from the neighborhoods) to the global level (comprising delegates from each *superregional coordination board*, cf. Sec. 7.1.2).

Each local association and each peer project that wants to undertake activities that would affect others (outside the association/project) in non-trivial ways would be expected to inform the most suitable—i.e., the smallest—information board about their plans to ensure that all stakeholders (or their delegates) know what is going on. A conflict occurs when stakeholders object to a planned activity but the project is not ready to modify its plans in a way that is acceptable to all.

Information boards might agree on a protocol for dealing with conflicts that the involved parties fail to resolve among themselves; for example, by referring such conflicts to an *arbitration board* that tries to mediate a solution that is acceptable to all involved parties. As a general guiding principle, arbitration boards should probably strive for rough consensus, meaning that plans will not be realized if some of the stakeholders have objections that cannot be addressed; but exceptions are conceivable, for example, if an action is of great importance for the people who want it and the objecting stakeholders are less severely affected.

Information and arbitration boards will also be able to redirect conflicts to a higher or lower level that they consider more appropriate due to more or fewer people being actually involved in a conflict. And delegates in information boards will probably keep themselves informed about what is going on in the information boards one level below their own, so the higher-level information board can take over a conflict if there are delegates for people who feel that they, too, are involved.

In many cases there will be "meta-conflicts" about who is or isn't a stakeholder, i.e., whether people that object to other people's decisions are sufficiently affected to intervene. Information boards will probably define guidelines to identify stakeholders (you are affected if actions of others modify or endanger your quality of life in a non-trivial way—you would be affected by a new building that obscures your rooms, but not by one that merely changes your view, unless the view is one of the major features of your room and would be ruined, etc.) Still, such meta-conflicts will remain and dealing with them will be an important part of the conflict resolution process.

The members of arbitration boards should be chosen among all the people living in the respective area, they should not speak for any specific group of people (as the delegates in the other kinds of boards do). Some large current peer projects have similar conflict resolution mechanisms which might serve as models, notably the dispute resolution process[1] of the Wikipedia with its Arbitration Committee[2] as last resort.

In case of non-compliance, when projects or people fail to report relevant plans to the information board or if they don't comply with arbitration decisions, the usual sanctioning mechanisms will come into play (cf. Sec. 5.6.1). Should *flaming and shunning* be unsuccessful, various variants and grades of *exclusion* and *strategic non-cooperation* are possible: people might be refused access to the services of the *local meta-projects;* projects can be excluded from the *prosumer association* they are in; regional and superregional cooperation with a defaulting local association could be suspended; people can always refuse to contribute to projects or to acquire their products.

While even more drastic measures such as intervention by

1 http://en.wikipedia.org/wiki/Wikipedia:Resolving_disputes

2 http://en.wikipedia.org/wiki/Wikipedia:Arbitration_Committee

force are conceivable, we doubt that they will be necessary. In an economy where cooperation is essential, the most severe forms of *exclusion* and *strategic non-cooperation* will probably be enough to deal with any defectors.

7.3. Education and Learning

In a market economy, the amount and prestige of education, especially formal education, a person receives is an important factor in the competition for jobs and positions. Without this competition, education and learning will probably take a different shape, focused more on acquiring the knowledge and skills you want or need rather than on spending certain amounts of time in institutions and passing through a specified set of courses. For sure, these two aspects of education are not necessarily in conflict—but neither do they fit together as closely as might seem.

As, for example, John Holt (1989) points out, learning is not an isolated activity; it is a continuous, interactive process that seems to be most successful when it happens in the context of daily life. Learning is mainly a process of figuring things out, a process of discovery (just like science). You learn best if a have a reason for doing something, if you want to know or be able to do something—small children learn to talk quite effortlessly in this way, without any need for schools or other formal institutions. Generally, learning seems to works best while doing something "real," if only as a game or experiment.

The best teaching method, therefore, is to *support* other people figuring things out for themselves, doing them by themselves, solving problems they like to have solved (or are just curious about); teaching is not a process of piping knowledge into somebody else's head. The best learning environment is the real world: to help children learn, Holt recommends to make things accessible for them so they can explore them and try them out; to make it possible for children to observe others (older children or adults) while doing what they do and to help them doing it, if such help can be of use. Both adults and children learn best when they really want to learn, either out of a genuine interest or because they need skills and knowledge for any activity they are doing or would like to do.

In the market economy, the need to acquire degrees and titles to better compete makes such an open concept of learning hard to realize; and the formal framework of schools and universities prepares young people for the formal framework of the business world. In a peer economy, neither of these concerns applies, rendering obsolete the formal framework of education as we know it today.

The architect Christopher Alexander, whose work *A Pattern Language* (1977) develops a method for creating livable (if somewhat traditional) architecture but in doing so covers much more, gives some impressions of how these activities might be organized instead:

Network of learning: "Instead of the lock-step of compulsory schooling in a fixed place, work in piecemeal ways to decentralize the process of learning and enrich it through contact with many places and people all over the city: workshops, teachers at home or walking through the city, professionals willing to take on the young as helpers, older children teaching younger children, museums, youth groups traveling, scholarly seminars, industrial workshops, old people, and so on." (Alexander et al., 1977, Pattern 18, p. 102)

University as a marketplace: "Establish the university as a marketplace of higher education. As a social conception this means that the university is open to people of all ages, on a full-time, part-time, or course by course basis. Anyone can offer a class. Anyone can take a class. Physically, the university marketplace has a central crossroads where its main buildings and offices are, and the meeting rooms and labs ripple out from this crossroads—at first concentrated in small buildings along pedestrian streets and then gradually becoming more dispersed and mixed with the town." (Pattern 43, p. 234)

Master and apprentices: "Arrange the work in every workgroup, industry, and office, in such a way that work and learning go forward hand in hand. Treat every piece of work as an opportunity for learning. To this end, organize work around a tradition of masters and apprentices: and support this form of social organization with a division of the workspace into spatial clusters—one for each master and his [or her] apprentices—where they can work and meet together." (Pattern 83, p. 414f)

Of course, local associations will decide for themselves how to arrange learning and education, and it is quite possible that they decide to continue the current formal arrangements, at least for some time. But we would be surprised if they did so in the long run, since, even though this might appear to be reasonable now, it will hardly be reasonable then.

7.4. Creative Works and Other Freely Sharable Goods

There are many things that can be shared freely (everything that can be encoded as information). Hence, according to the tendency of peer production to *share what you can* (Sec. 4.4.1) we may assume that they will generally be available without restriction to anyone who wants them. This does not mean, however, that their creation cannot be recognized as a contribution within the task auctioning system of a peer project or local association that wants to have them. We can expect that writing a book that is to be used for teaching (for example) will be recognized as a contribution just as well as giving a course where this textbook is used.

There is a risk that projects will stall the creation of such freely sharable goods, hoping that other projects will create them first—after all, once such a book has been created, it can be used by anyone giving a course, not just the ordering project. But several factors make us doubt that such stalling will be a serious problem. It would be silly for a project to stall if the others do the same, since this would prevent any activities for which they need the work in question. And projects working on similar topics will tend to keep each other informed about their activities so as to avoid unnecessary duplication of effort. Projects interested in the same work might also decide to explicitly join forces by founding an independent project for creating it, sharing the effort required for this project among themselves.

In any case, projects that only take without ever giving back are likely to attract attention, causing embarrassment and loss of reputation to their members. Conversely, positive reputation for creating a work will go to the creators, not to users.

This task auctioning approach, however, works best for works that are needed in the context of a larger project, such as software or textbooks, manuals, and other kinds of nonfictional works. It is harder to imagine for literature, music or movies. Such works are not usually produced "on order," and, while they are enjoyed and appreciated, are not "needed" for any practical purpose.

Does this mean that such works might no longer be created in a peer economy when their creation is not honored with money or as weighted labor? This is certainly a point we do not have to worry about. People have always, and will always produce creative works. Not because they want to make money, but because they have time on their hand and a story to tell or a feeling to express. Or because they want to increase their fame and reputation and hope to attract lots of ardent admirers of their preferred gender(s). There are many good reasons for being creative, and most of them are unrelated to the necessity to earn money that dominates current society. Far from stopping creativity, a peer economy will give it more space to flourish, since artists are no longer constrained by the pressure to be marketable and since most people will probably have more time to spend as they like and fewer things to worry about.

Nevertheless, the people living in a peer economy *can* recognize the authors, musicians, and movie makers they like, beyond the increase in attention and reputation that automatically follows from being an appreciated artist. While such works can hardly be made "on order" and thus auctioned as tasks to handle, they can still be recognized as valuable contributions *after* they have been created.

The people living in a local association can reserve a certain amount of weighted labor to honor artists living in their area, by recognizing their creative work as contributions for their local meta-project (cf. Sec. 5.3). This would mean that everybody else would have to work very slightly more to organize the public services and infrastructure required by the association, while the recognized artists would be freed from participation in these tasks, giving them more free time to create further works. Of course, such a recognition will generally come only *post hoc,* after an artist has already finished one successful work—but this holds for market recognition of such works just as well and will hardly be a serious hindrance.

To decide which works to recognize in this way, both popular success (music which made it to the top of the charts, most frequently read books) or "artistic value" (as judged by a jury of experts) can serve as criteria. Preferably local associations will honor works that satisfy either criterion, recognizing mainstream success but also giving avant-garde, unconventional artists a chance. They will probably recognize creative works as a fixed amount of weighted labor depending on the kind and size of a work, since the amount of labor that actually went into creating a work will hardly be known after it has been completed and since this labor cannot be auctioned and hence not "weighted" anyway.

7.5. Styles of Production

As a general tendency, peer prosumers often seem to prefer products that are *modular, functional,* and *elegant.*

Products that are *modular,* that can be broken down into smaller modules or components which can be produced independently before being assembled into a whole, fit better into the peer mode of production than complex, convoluted products, since they make the tasks to be handled by a peer project more manageable. Projects can build upon modules produced by others and they can set as their own (initial) goal the production of a specific module, especially if components can be used stand-alone as well as in combination. The Unix philosophy of providing lots of small specialized tools that can be combined in versatile ways is probably the oldest expression in software of this modular style.

The stronger emphasis on modularity is another phenomenon that follows from the differences between market production and peer production. Market producers have to prevent their competitors from copying or integrating their products and methods of production so as not to lose their competitive advantage. In the peer mode, re-use by others is good and should be encouraged, since it increases your reputation and the likelihood of others giving something back to you.

Peer producers jointly produce for their own use, which explains their tendency to put *functionality* first. In the market, non-functional differences often are the only way to gain a competitive edge; in peer production there is no need for such distinctions. Peer producers certainly care about *form*, as shown by the innumerable *skins* and *templates* that change the appearance of many popular free software solutions, but putting form over function will hardly do—nobody would bother to "skin" a software that does not do what they want it to do.

Elegance is often closely related to functionality and to a certain simplicity that benefits modularity and re-use—"Elegance is the attribute of being unusually effective and simple," the Wikipedia (2007) defines. Free software producers tend to admire elegance especially, but not only, in design. Eric Raymond (2001, Lesson 13) expresses this by quoting Antoine de Saint-Exupéry: "Perfection (in design) is achieved not when there is nothing more to add, but rather when there is nothing more to take away."

Modularity not only facilitates decentralized innovation, but should also help to increase the longevity of products and components. Capitalism has developed a throw-away culture where things are often discarded when they break (instead of being repaired), or when one aspect of them is no longer up-to-date or in fashion. In a peer economy, the tendency in such cases will be to replace just a single component instead of the whole product, since this will generally be the most labor-efficient option (compared to getting a new product, but also to manually repairing the old one).

The logical equivalent to the *modularity* of products is the *decentralization* of production processes. Current peer production processes tend to be extremely decentralized, since they take place over the Internet and participants are often distributed over the whole globe (or the parts of it where reliable Internet access is common and affordable). Future peer projects that produce material items will be stronger tied to places where the physical production takes place. Probably this will often lead to a combination of global cooperation for designing products and local production for physically manufacturing them.

But decentralization will hardly become extreme since many production processes require a sufficiently large scale to be efficient—it would be impossible or at least pointless for each village to have their own computer chip factory, since setting up and maintaining the necessary facilities requires a huge effort which will reasonably be shared by a high number of people. Trying to minimize their efforts, peer producers will find suitable trade-offs between production effort and transportation effort.

Still, physical production in a peer economy will certainly be far more decentralized than in the market economy, where the effects of market competition favor centralization by eliminating most players. Also, regardless of our warnings about overestimating "personal fabricators," recent technological developments go in a direction that shifts the balance in favor of smaller-scale production. Fabbing and similar technologies will support localized production in so far as they are available, and there is no need for fabricators to be "personal" to be useful. Existing technologies such as *rapid manufacturing* (Hopkinson et al., 2006) already allow flexible industrial production in small series and might be just as useful for a peer project or a local community as a personal fabricator would be for a single person.

The relative preference for decentralization will probably also affect areas such as *energy.* Even more important than the local availability of energy sources will be their *sustainability.* Peer projects and local associations will prefer energy sources that are *used* (such as solar energy, biomass, wind power, or hydropower) instead of *used up* (such as oil). If not for the sensible reason that they want to preserve and protect the environment they are living in, they will do so for the simple reason that non-renewable resources, if still in high demand, will draw enormous prices in the distribution pool as soon as they become scarce. Energy sources with a risk of potentially high damage such as nuclear power will hardly be employed, since they will be blocked by stakeholders who would have to live with the risk (cf. Sec. 7.2).

Regarding *means of transport,* local associations will probably prefer to provide for non-rival solutions—i.e., solutions that scale efficiently instead of deteriorating if the number of users increases—since this is the most effective and fair way of providing transportation infrastructure and services for their inhabitants. Cars in cities and for long-distance travel are a notorious failure in this respect, as the existence of traffic jams, car-related pollution, and lack of parking demonstrates. Instead, local meta-projects will mainly cater for public transport (buses, trams, metros, trains, etc.) for densely populated areas such as cities and for long-distance travel.

Personal cars will remain popular in rural areas where the population is too distributed for effective public transportation systems. Even there, a good and versatile public transport system or a comparable solution would be important to bring mobility to children and old or disabled people. For short and medium distances, non-obtrusive personal vehicles such as bicycles will be a good solution everywhere. And to cover situations where other means of transport are inadequate or absent, local communities and neighborhoods can provide shared *community cars/vehicles.*

8. Concerns

Prior to concluding this text, we will discuss questions and concerns that might arise in regard to the peer economy.

8.1. How to Handle Contributions?

8.1.1. What About People Who Cannot Contribute?

The peer economy, by default, is about effort sharing—people jointly contributing to a common goal that none of them could reach alone. But not everyone will be able to contribute. There are various good reasons to exempt people from contributing—children, people who are too old to work, people who are ill or disabled, pregnant women, parents with young children, ... The people living in a peer economy will need to deal with such exemptions: (1) they will need to decide who is exempted but eligible for goods; (2) they will need allocation models allowing exempted people access to goods without having to contribute anything in return; and (3) they will need to redistribute the effort necessary to produce these goods among the remaining contributors.

When discussing the allocation of natural resources in a peer economy, we noted an interesting effect of auctioning resources that cannot be distributed on a flat-rate basis (cf. Sec. 5.5.3): the effort that the winner of a resource auction has to contribute in order to get the resource will make all the other goods distributed in the same *distribution pool* slightly cheaper, since no effort has been spent to create the resource (it is not the result of human labor). Distributing products to people who don't have to contribute any effort has the inverse effect. The effort necessary for the production of these goods would be redistributed among all the people contributing to the pool—all the goods distributed through the pool would become slightly more expensive.

This offers a simple and flexible solution for question 3 (how to redistribute the effort), provided that the people participating in a pool can agree on answers to the other two questions. Again we can look at the issue of resource allocation for inspiration: above we noted that the effect of resource distribution on the cost of all other goods means that the people sharing their resources in the same pool will have to reach an agreement on which resources to consider *available,* and proposed a bottom-up mechanism for making such decisions (Sec. 5.6.3.2). This also holds when a distribution pool is used to redistribute effort for exempted persons. The same bottom-up decision making process can therefore be extended to answer the two remaining questions: how to define conditions for exemption and how to handle the allocation of goods that cannot be freely shared (cf. Sec. 4.4.2) in such cases.

A possible approach to the second question would be to consider non-contributors as "average" contributors: to calculate the average amount of weighted labor the contributors have put into the distribution pool over the last year (or so) and to entitle each non-contributor to choose among the results of the project as if she had contributed this average amount of labor. Alternatively, the involved local associations might decide to grant access to ex-contributors based on their *personal* average of contributions over their active years. This would allow people who had preferred to work harder in order to get more, or more expensive, things, to continue their standard of living.

The exact details will have to be agreed on within and between the involved local associations, and they will certainly lead to some occasional grumbling by either non-contributors or contributors (or both). However, we assume that, as a tendency, these decisions will be fair to both contributors and non-contributors. There will hardly be enough non-contributors to press unfair conditions on the contributors; and the contributors will know that they will sooner or later become non-contributors themselves, more likely than not, so it would by silly for them to treat non-contributors badly.

Also, while people and local associations participating in the pool won't be able to opt out from the reached agreements (since the necessary effort is automatically redistributed among all the contributions to the pool), they can always complement them with their own alternative redistribution schemes if they consider them insufficient. The inhabitants of a specific local association might prefer to consider further persons exempted or to handle allocation more generously. If they fail to change the criteria for the whole pool, they can still decide to apply these more generous conditions within their own area, distributing the additional necessary effort among themselves.

One thing that might be self-evident but is still noteworthy because it differs from current practice is that an exemption from contributing will hardly be a *prohibition* to contribute. In free software projects, nobody checks your age to decide whether you are "old enough" or "young enough" to contribute, and we see no reasons why future peer projects should introduce such tests. People triggering an exemption clause will not be *expected* to contribute, but they will be *allowed* to do so, if they feel like it.

The involved local associations will have to decide whether to treat such actual contributions as *additional* to the "virtual" contributions assumed for an exempted person (so you can get more goods if you contribute somewhat though you are exempted), or whether to consider them as *alternative* (so it is the maximum of your actual and your virtual contributions that counts, not their sum). A good compromise might be to treat such voluntary contributions as additional, but to recognize only 50% of their effort.

8.1.2. What About People Who Don't Want to Contribute?

What if there are people who are perfectly able to contribute and not exempted, but who refuse to contribute anything and still expect to get a portion of the non-sharable results produced by a project?

We don't suppose that this would be a frequent situation—it would be pretty silly for people to expect others to work for their benefit, while refusing to give anything back. If some people do, they can of course try to convince the others to work on their behalf, but we suppose that they would need good arguments to win them over. It is possible that they can make a good case why they, too, should be exempted. But unless they can, they will probably have to choose whether they want to participate in a project or association (with both the requirements and benefits this entails) or whether they don't. Nobody will be forced to cooperate with others, but if you refuse to cooperate with others, you can hardly expect them to cooperate with you.

This does not mean that you would have to starve if you refuse to cooperate. People might be well be (consciously) lax in controlling who has access to basic foodstuffs (such as available on a flat-rate basis); they might grant free access to lodgings that are being re-auctioned or that fail to attract anybody willing to live there; and they would certainly not refuse basic health care to anybody who needs it. But a life of non-cooperation would be much harder and less pleasant than a life of cooperation, and we doubt that many (if any) people would choose it.

In capitalism, the primary reason why people "drop out of the system" is that they have lost a job (or never held one) and sooner or later realize that their chances of finding a new one are so low that they just give up. Or people are unwilling to work for others. But in the peer economy, you don't need to find a job, you only have to choose among the tasks that need to be done, and there should always be some suitable ones. And you don't work *for* others, but *with* others, which is a big difference. Because of this, we would not be surprised if this problem never arises. But if it does, people will find suitable ways of dealing with it.

8.1.3. How to Decide Which Contributions to Accept?

We have assumed that projects whose results cannot be copied freely will often share the efforts necessary for production along with the benefits, requiring those who want to benefit to contribute their part to the overall effort (cf. Sec. 4.2). It is important that this requirement should be used only for effort sharing, it should not become an exclusion mechanism. It would be bad if people were prevented from benefiting from the material results of a project because they cannot contribute anything in return.

There are thus two goals that will sometimes be in conflict: on the one hand, projects will want to ensure that all tasks are handled well and reliably; on the other hand, people will need to be able to contribute in some way.

This problem should be alleviated through the existence of distribution pools as huge shared task auctioning systems (cf. Sec. 5.2). Such a shared auctioning system will offer a high variety of tasks, requiring widely varying skills and capabilities, so there should be a good choice of suitable tasks for everybody (especially since some tasks won't require any special skills at all, and since people can learn skills they don't yet possess).

Projects participating in a distribution pool will have reason to strive for a good balance between ensuring that the quality of contributions is high and between being overly picky about potential contributors. If they were to accept lousy contributions, they would risk their reputation and the success of their project, and in occasional cases even their health or their lives. But if they reject good contributions, waiting instead for others to come along, the relative value of the unassigned task in the labor weighting system will automatically go up, increasing the overall effort necessary to reach their goals.

One risk that must be taken seriously is that people's choices regarding what they do and the decisions of projects regarding whose contributions to prefer can be influenced by prejudices about which people are better at which tasks. People might consciously or subconsciously base their evaluations of actual or potential contributions somebody offers on irrelevant criteria such as her gender, "race," origin, or age. And people might base their decisions about which tasks they themselves want to handle on prejudices about what people "like them" are supposed to do (or to be good at), instead of letting their own interests and strengths prevail.

This is not only a problem for the affected person, since it restricts her choices and might reduce her happiness and her self-esteem, but also for the involved projects. Task auctioning systems will run more smoothly if everybody is able to choose freely among all the available tasks according to their own preferences; and the average quality of contributions will be higher if it is only the quality of contributions that determines which contributions are accepted, instead of prejudices about contributors.

It is thus in the best interest of everyone to try to reduce such prejudices as far as possible. Of course, this does not mean that they will never influence decisions, but it should be possible to largely reduce their effects, by spreading the knowledge that this problem exists and that it should be consciously counteracted, and by complaining about unfair decisions. The usual sanctioning mechanism of the peer economy ("flaming and shunning" and, if necessary, exclusion and strategic non-cooperation) can be applied against people or projects who refuse to overcome their prejudices.

Forking is another option: if a project is arbitrary or unfair in its dealings with potential contributors, they can always found their own alternative project; and due to the tendency to treat software, designs and other information as part of the commons ("Share what you can," cf. Sec. 4.4.1), the hurdles for doing so should not be too high. In many cases, it might also be possible to adapt the practice of the scientific community to perform *blind reviews,* where the quality of contributions (or the suitability of applications for any given task) is evaluated with all personal information about the contributor, and possibly about her prior occupations and activities, being hidden from the evaluators.

8.1.4. What About Tasks That Are Not Recognized as Contributions?

What about activities that are not distributed through any task auctioning systems? Isn't there a risk that such activities will still be distributed in a biased way, mainly to persons of one gender, for example?

In capitalism, there has long been a gender-specific division of work, where women were expected to do the housework, care for the kids and do other unpaid activities, while men were expected to earn the money for their family. While the part about "earning the money" has meanwhile been relaxed, it is still mainly women doing the unpaid domestic work (in addition to any paid jobs they are holding). Isn't there a risk that such an unfair division of work will be perpetuated into a peer economy?

Yes, this risk exists, and it will be up to the people living in the peer economy to deal with it. In so far as tasks are distributed by personal agreements instead of being auctioned, the peer economy does not in any way ensure that they will be distributed *fairly*. It will be up to the persons arranging such agreements to take care that they are fair and do not stipulate people's roles according to their gender or other irrelevant criteria. In the mentioned case, it would be up to the men to take care that they do not expect more of the women than they themselves are willing to give, and it would be up to the women to protest, and to refuse to partake in any unfair agreements (to "go on strike," if necessary) if the men fail to do so.

Also, it is possible to use task auctioning even within the context of individual households or groups of households to avoid the arbitrariness that individual agreements might impose. And if the people participating in any task auctioning system find that tasks are still distributed unevenly according to gender (or some other arbitrary criterion), they could decide to set up separate auctioning systems for women and men, thus inciting men to do tasks that so far have been mainly handled by women (since these tasks will be weighted higher in the "male" auctioning system), and vice versa.

The peer economy does not solve all problems by itself, but it gives the people better preconditions for solving them than they have now.

8.2. How to Handle Effort?

8.2.1. What About Huge or Uncertain Efforts?

Distribution pools (cf. Sec. 5.2) are a way of sharing effort between projects that allows you to get goods from many different projects without having to contribute to all of them. By providing a single shared system for the distribution of tasks and goods, distribution pools allow you and your project to produce goods for the benefit of others, and get in turn access to the goods produced by others, without requiring everyone to directly contribute to *all* of the projects whose products they like to have. This effort-sharing mechanism works by distributing goods produced by your project to people who want them and consider them "worth the effort," i.e., who are willing to contribute the same amount of effort (weighted labor) back to the pool so *you* can get some goods produced by others. This means that your effort will only be recognized after you have finished and distributed goods that others want to have.

What if a huge preparatory effort is required until any goods can be produced, say for building an intricate factory such as necessary for producing microprocessors or other computer equipment? What if it is initially uncertain if your efforts will indeed lead to any usable goods, say if the technical feasibility of your plans cannot be determined without further research or experiments? In such cases, it is quite possible that there won't be normal projects willing to undertake the necessary work. If an uncertain attempt fails, the project members would have wasted all their efforts; otherwise, they might have to wait a long time until their effort turns into usable goods (for others, and therefore for themselves).

In such cases, it might be up to *local associations* or *prosumer associations* to pitch in and to mitigate the risk or the delay by distributing it among their members. The inhabitants of a local association (especially a larger one such as a *region*) might decide to add the tasks necessary for a huge or uncertain undertaking to its *local meta-project* (cf. Sec. 5.3). This would mean that initially, while preparations or research are under way, the inhabitants of the association will all have to work slightly more, since the required effort is distributed evenly among them. If the undertaking is successful, this effect can later be recovered by distributing the produced goods in the usual way both inside and (through a distribution pool) outside the local association—inhabitants not interested in the produced goods will now have to work slightly less, until the advanced effort has been recovered.

Prosumer associations (cf. Sec. 5.4) or other groups of projects can advance effort in the same way, if they consider an activity useful or necessary for their purposes. In this case, advance effort will be added to the tasks the participating projects have to handle, so everything produced by them will temporarily become slightly more expensive (as measured in production effort). If production is successful, their production effort will temporarily decrease, since they now benefit from the effort contributed by others in return for the effort they had advanced before.

Usually the members of a local or prosumer association will only be willing to safeguard production in this way if sufficiently many of them take an interest in the project in question (as potential users, contributors, or both) and if they consider the people willing to undertake the work as competent and trustworthy—otherwise they will hardly be willing to take the risk of having wasted effort if the undertaking ends in failure, especially if the successful completion of a project is uncertain. If they consider the chances of success sufficiently high, they might also safeguard an undertaking without a personal interest in the outcome, knowing they themselves might some day benefit from such mutual safeguarding.

If neither prosumer nor local associations are willing to safeguard a huge or uncertain project, production may still take place if there are sufficiently many contributors willing to take the risk, either in hope of future recognition (if their activity finally leads to useful goods) or just "for the sake of it." Also, potential consumers interested in getting something produced can decide to support the producers by pre-recognizing their effort (as if they had already received the goods), even if they don't want to get involved into the actual production process.

Efforts that don't result in any usable goods (or not immediately, at least), such as basic research, are best coordinated by local or prosumer associations, so the necessary effort (though not the actual work) will be shared among all. But if no association sees the benefits of a research project, it is still quite possible that there will be people willing to do the work (even though their efforts won't be recognized as such), out of interest in the outcome or in hope of increasing their reputation. We suppose that the effort people will have to spend for co-producing the infrastructure, services, and other goods they want to have won't be that high, leaving them lots of time and energy to pursue other activities.

8.2.2. Effort Shifting

What if you are not exempted from contributing (cf. Sec. 8.1.1), but would prefer not to contribute anything for a few months or years, so you can spend this time for traveling, relaxing, or some private project of your own, without distractions?

The peer economy works by distributing the effort necessary to produce goods among the people who want to have them. Therefore, shifting effort to some earlier or later time is not trivial. You cannot simply save effort for later by contributing more in the present and claiming some goods in return for it in the future—in general, effort is needed when goods are being produced, not later or earlier. Short delays will hardly be a problem—people won't mind if a few weeks or months pass until you acquire goods for the effort you have contributed (or, if they trust you, the other way around). But if you want to advance or postpone your required part of the effort for longer periods of time, some explicit agreements are necessary.

Local associations are in a good position to make such agreements. If some members temporarily contribute more than required to a *local meta-project,* everybody else will have to contribute slightly less; if the advance-contributed effort is later claimed, the others will have to contribute slightly more. As long as the shifted effort is only a small proportion of the overall effort required for the meta-project, this should not be a problem and it should all sum up in the end.

Hence, local associations might decide to grant their inhabitants the possibility of *sabbaticals,* of periods where they don't have to contribute anything, by allowing them to contribute some more effort than required and later to claim services and any other goods in return for the advanced effort. If local associations organize their activities in the context of a distribution pool, as we suppose (cf. Sec. 5.3.3), this advanced effort can later be spend on *any* goods and resources distributed through the pool, not just on those organized by the local association. For example, if you have advanced 1000 weighted hours and your local association requires 600 weighted hours as yearly contributions, you won't have to contribute anything for a year and you'll still have 400 weighted hours left to get other goods.

So as not to jeopardize the smooth running of the meta-project, local associations might impose limits on the effort that can be pre-contributed in this way (say, no more than two years of average contributions). We suppose that they will be quite willing to grant this option, since many people will like the possibility of sabbaticals.

8.3. What About Migration?

We stated above (Sec. 2.2) that cooperation in a peer context is always voluntary, never coerced. If people want to leave a peer project or a local association, they are free to go. This freedom to leave or to "fork" is an essential aspect of peer cooperation—but it would become effectively void if there were no places to go to. In case of normal peer projects, this is less of an issue, since you can create new "places" at will, by founding a new project and inviting others to join you. But for local associations (cf. Sec. 5.3) the situation is different: since local associations take physical space on Earth, founding a new one will generally not be an option, since there won't be suitable spaces left.

In local associations, the *right to leave* thus needs to be complemented with a *right to join*, or it won't be effective. Local associations adhering to the spirit of peer cooperation will not only let their inhabitants go if they want to go, but they will also let others join the association if they want to. Indeed, in a society based on commons and not on property, it would be hard to justify why an area should be treated as the exclusive property of the people who happen to be born there.

Of course, local associations will expect potential immigrants to contribute their share to the organization of local infrastructure and public services just like everyone else; and they will expect them to make any preparations that are necessary for doing so (such as learning the local language). Such requirements are reasonable and hardly problematic, but they alone might be insufficient to handle migration. What can popular local associations do to avoid being overrun by immigrants?

8.3.1. Auctioning of Grounds and Houses as Regulation Mechanism

Once more, auctioning can come to the rescue. Auctioning grounds and houses will make living in popular places less attractive (due to higher prices), while increasing the attractiveness of unpopular places. This will only work if grounds and houses in both popular and less popular places are assigned through the same auctioning system, since, in the peer economy, it is only the *relative* prices that are modified through auctioning—the effort required for building and maintaining houses stays the same, but it is distributed in a different way. But as long as the grounds and houses of sufficiently many local associations are allocated through the same *distribution pool* (cf. Sec. 5.2), this will hardly be a problem, since such distribution pools should be large enough to comprise both popular and less popular local associations.

In this way, potential immigrants will think twice before moving into very popular (and thus high-priced) areas. This benefits local associations that are popular immigration targets: it saves them from becoming overcrowded or else having to resort to dubious coercive measures to keep others out. The advantage for other, less popular associations lies in the effort-redistribution effect of auctioning: the higher prices for grounds and housing in other areas automatically cause the prices of all the other goods and resources distributed through the pool (including grounds and housing in their own area) to go down.

This effect of course also means that the people living in a popular area will have to pay (contribute) more for housing than they would otherwise. This effect can be mitigated by granting more favorable conditions to the locals of any specific community than to recently immigrated people. One option would be to calculate the additional effort that the people living in a popular local community have to contribute due to their grounds and houses being auctioned openly in the distribution pool instead of just among themselves; and to give half the effort back to the community. This effort could be distributed evenly among all the locals (say, among everybody who lived there five years ago), granting each of them a certain amount of weighted hours that they can spend for housing or other goods and resources from the pool (cf. Section A.4 in the mathematical appendix for a more detailed treatment). The various local associations participating in a distribution pool will have to agree on the exact terms of such an arrangement. This might involve some negotiation due to the differing interests of popular and less popular places, but in the end it shouldn't be too hard to reach an agreement, since both benefit from a functioning system.

8.3.2. Migration of Non-Contributors

What about the migration of people who are exempted from contributing (cf. Sec. 8.1.1)? In general, this should not be a problem, since we noted above that it makes sense for all the local associations participating in a distribution pool to agree on common conditions for exemptions. Thus, the effort spent on behalf of non-contributors will be evenly distributed among all contributors to the pool, regardless of where they live. However, if some local associations have agreed on more generous conditions in regard to non-contributors in their own area, they might decide not to grant these conditions to newcomers who have made no or few contributions to their local meta-project.

Only if non-contributors want to move between local associations participating in *different* distribution pools, things become more complicated, since the members of the target distribution pool might be unwilling to work on behalf of people who never have contributed, and probably never will. This will probably be another factor promoting the emergence of a single global distribution pool, since people will like to have unimpeded global mobility, regardless of whether they can (still) contribute or not.

However, as long as this does not happen, different distribution pools can still negotiate agreements on how to handle migration in such cases. For example, they might keep a tally of how much effort the members of a distribution pool spend on behalf of exempted persons immigrated from other pools, and balance the difference from time to time. This would ensure full mobility even across different distribution pools.

8.4. Won't There Be Need for Further Laws and Standards?

Won't a peer production–based society need further regulation mechanisms beyond those we have already discussed? We do not think so.

In market-based societies, regulation mechanisms such as laws and standards are essential to constrain the effects of the market. The consequence of market competition (cf. Sec. 6.1.4) is that the *worst practice* becomes a *de facto* standard all the others are compelled to follow. If a company manages to reduce its production costs by treating its workers badly, by forgoing safety precautions, or by damaging or endangering the environment, it puts strong pressure on its competitors to engage in similar practices, since they have to adjust their own production costs in order to remain competitive. Therefore laws and standards regulating how workers and the environment are to be treated are crucial. They are the only way to make the worst—i.e., the *de facto* standard—less bad than it would be otherwise.

The peer economy is far more self-regulating in this respect. There is no need to enforce labor standards on projects, since it is the people in a project who decide on their own labor conditions. People will hardly impose bad or dangerous conditions for their own work; and if they hope to find volunteers through a task auctioning system, it would be pointless to do so, since this would reduce the number of volunteers and hence cause the cost of the task to go up instead of down (as already mentioned in Section 6.1.4).

Similarly, there is no need for peer projects to adapt practices that harm or endanger the environment, regardless of what other projects do; and projects still doing so will likely see their reputation and attractiveness sink, making it reasonable for them to change their behavior for purely selfish reasons. The effects of market competition reward those that do bad, as long as they can get away with it. The peer economy, on the other hand, favors those that behave well, that "do the right thing," since you need to attract contributors who will care for their own *reputation* and therefore for yours.

Moreover, prosumer associations can define *guidelines* that projects participating in an association are supposed to follow (cf. Sec. 5.4.3). This will help to ensure that suitable standards are kept by most projects, as projects violating these guidelines will probably have more difficulties in finding contributors and consumers. They also risk being excluded from the prosumer association, losing the benefits of horizontal coordination it offers (cf. Sec. 5.4).

Finally, whenever people want to do something that seriously affects the lives of others, the mechanisms for *stakeholder involvement* and *conflict resolution* (Sec. 7.2) come into play. Activities that endanger others or the environment they live in are likely to be stopped at this stage, if not before. The peer economy does have regulation mechanisms for such situations; they just don't need a state or other "sovereign" to be effective.

This also covers what need for other laws there might arise. Law is essentially a conflict resolution mechanism. If there is no conflict, if everybody involved agrees to an activity, there is no reason to "outlaw" it and to prosecute it as a crime.

Of course, the conflict resolution institutions will need to deal with and sanction defectors—people who violate or harm others or who disregard the wishes and decisions of stakeholders in other ways; and people who use threats or deceit to make others agree to something they would not otherwise agree to. And they will need to take care to detect and handle conflicts that are not apparent (e.g., because the victim has been intimidated into remaining silent). When there is a conflict, society might have to intervene to make sure that it is resolved in a fair manner and that one side does not lose because they are weaker or otherwise disadvantaged. But when there is no conflict, there is no need for law.

8.5. Won't Such a Society Revert to a Market Economy?

Is there a risk that a peer production–based society would not be stable, but would revert to a market-based economy sooner or later?

For one, let's make it clear that this would not be a *risk* but a *possibility*—if people prefer an alternative mode of production instead of the dominant one, they certainly have the right to choose it. But we don't think it very likely that they would prefer the market economy. The market requires people who sell their own labor capacity; if there is nobody willing to sell her labor capacity, no market-based production is possible (aside from very limited forms of barter exchange which wouldn't be a serious alternative).

But when given the choice between cooperating freely with others to produce what they want or else submitting themselves to the command of others in order to earn money which then allows them to buy some of the goods they want (provided they manage to get hold of a suitable position and that somebody else is producing those goods), we doubt that many people would choose the second option. It would be less efficient because of the additional indirection and the various ways in which the necessity to remain competitive distorts market production (cf. Sec. 6.1). It would restrict their freedom since they have to subordinate themselves to the command of others. And it would certainly be less fun.

Moreover, the laws of market competition make sure that market participants are never really in control, regardless of their position in the production process. Even if it is you who command others and not the other way around, you are not free in your decisions. All you can do is to try to find out what the market postulates and implement it as good as you can, or else to fail. Today, these laws of the market are often perceived as "laws of nature" that seem to be as inevitable as the laws of gravity, and therefore they are accepted. We doubt that people would choose to voluntary re-submit themselves to these laws (and thereby resign most of their freedom in regard to future choices) once they have realized that they are not "laws of nature" at all, but merely artifacts of a specific system of production.

Today, the market only works because most people are *forced* to sell their labor capacity, or else to forgo most of their needs and desires and live a life of destitution and hardship. The market is dominant since there hasn't been a suitable alternative, but the emergence of peer production is changing this.

For sure, there will be defenders of the current market-and-state system—especially those who have power or privilege to lose—that will do everything they can to prevent people from realizing that they *have* a choice between peer production and market production. They will use tricks, propaganda, laws, and possibly force in an attempt to stop the spreading of peer production. But if and when the proponents of peer production win this struggle, if and when a sufficient number of people realize that peer production *is* an alternative, we doubt that the market will stand a chance.

8.6. Aren't There Many Variants to the Proposed Model?

Aren't there many ways in which an actual peer economy might and will be different from the model we have proposed in this text? There certainly are.

Our goal was to find out whether a society where peer production is the primary mode of production is possible, and how it might be organized. For this it was necessary to develop one model—or a family of models—of such a society, but it was not necessary (and would have been infeasible) to develop *all possible* models. Indeed, we have often enough mentioned throughout the text that there might be other possibilities.

In case that some aspects of the proposed model seem arbitrary, we would like to point out the underlying principles that guided our choices. We attempted to find sensible solutions to the problems that the people cooperating in peer mode will face—trying, in so far as possible, to regard these problems from the perspective of somebody living in a peer economy, not from somebody living in capitalism. We tried to look for solutions that correspond to the philosophy of peer production as we can observe it today: solutions that emphasize commons and sharing; where reputation matters and status doesn't; solutions that rely on free cooperation and do not require coercion of any kind. We tried to look for those solutions that might seem most sensible to the people living in such a society, and that will work well for everybody, without requiring people to be idealists or to fit into other patterns that might not be appropriate for them.

Actually, there have not been as many choices in finding the proposed model as one might think. In many cases, possible alternatives come to mind, but if you think them through you will notice that they would not work, or that they would have some unpleasant side effects. A society is not like a heap of stuff you can pile up in any way you like; it is more like a bridge where you must be careful where to place the pillars and how to form and compound all parts, lest it fall down.

9. Conclusion: The Development of a Peer Economy

We started this text by asking how far the potential of *peer production* extends—production based on sharing and cooperation instead of property and competition. We have found that there is no reason why peer production should remain limited to the niche of information goods where it first emerged. We have seen that people can coordinate their wishes as producers with their needs as consumers by *automating* unpleasant activities away; by making tasks more *fun;* and by weighting less pleasant or less popular tasks higher *(task auctioning),* allowing everybody to choose their own trade-off between the tasks they want to do and the time they are willing to spend on them. We have seen that they can distribute the results of their cooperation by *freely sharing what can be shared* (such as information), and by distributing non-sharable products among the contributors according to their preferences and wishes. They might use various models such as *flat rates, flat allocation, customized production* with effort-based accounting, or *preference weighting (product auctioning)* to organize this internal sharing in a fair way without restricting anybody's choices.

People can initiate and join any such *peer projects* to jointly produce the things they like to have and/or to do the things they like to do. Peer projects can join their forces in large *distribution pools* that use a shared auctioning system for tasks, products, and resources, allowing everybody access to a wide range of goods without having to contribute to a multiplicity of projects. Aside from such interest-based cooperation, the people in any given area can cooperate locally, forming *local meta-projects* to coordinate the public services and infrastructure they desire to have in their area. And projects active in the same sector of production will often choose to coordinate their activities and to share their experiences in *prosumer associations.* Thus, a society based on peer production will be characterized by manifold cooperation both *within* and *between* peer projects.

We have seen that a society is possible where all economic activity is arranged in this way. In this society, production will be driven by demand and not by profit. There will be no need to sell anything and hence no unemployment; competition will be more a game than a struggle for survival; there won't be a distinction between people with capital and those without, or between people living in a center and those living in the periphery. In this society, it would be silly to keep your ideas and knowledge secret instead of sharing them; and scarcity will no longer be a precondition of economic success, but a problem to be worked around.

All this is possible, but will it become real?

This is a question which we cannot seriously answer since it concerns events that have not yet occurred. We cannot predict the future. But we can look at the past and present for indicators. And there are positive indicators.

One is that the formulas preaching capitalism as the solution to all the world's problems ring more and more hollow by the day. There is the material destitution affecting more and more people; the widening gap between rich and poor people and rich and poor countries; the increasing feeling of people being left out, encouraging hate and fanaticism or resignation and despair; the oncoming environmental disasters. People might not yet realize that capitalism is the root cause of these problems, but more and more of them probably do not *seriously* believe that it can solve them either. So far they might be hesitant to admit this fact, even to themselves, since they do not know of better alternatives, and an unfounded hope is still preferable to hopelessness. But as soon as you realize that there *is* an alternative, there is no reason to persist in this self-delusion.

Another positive indicator is the astonishing and unpredicted success of free software and open content, the first area where peer production started to become apparent. Especially, when we realize that the three arguments which applied to the formation of free software apply here as well: the *ethical* argument (think Richard Stallman), the *practical* argument (think Apache Foundation), and the *fun* argument (think Linus Torvalds).

Stallman's *ethical argument* (cf. Stallman, 2002, Chap. 1) is that a system that prevents you from helping your neighbor (by sharing your software with her) is wrong, and that it is absurd if you cannot change the software you are using to fit your needs (or those of others). Stallman argues that a system that is absurd and ethically wrong must be rejected and changed, explaining why he favors free software and rejects all property in software.

The same argument can be made for peer production instead of market production in general. It is absurd that people have to live in miserable circumstances just because they don't manage to find paid work (which, in many cases, isn't even of real use to anybody); it is wrong that children have to starve even though there is enough to eat for everybody. Markets cannot solve these problems (they create them), but peer production can. We have a choice between market production and peer production, but if we want to behave ethically, we cannot choose the former.

The Apache Software Foundation[1] represents the pragmatic case for free software. Their flagship project, the *Apache HTTP Server*[2], has been the most popular Web server since 1996. This server was originally developed by a group of webmasters who found that they all had similar needs and problems, and who realized that by cooperating and freely sharing the resulting software they could address them in the most efficient way (cf. Apache Software Foundation, 2005).

Their reasons for cooperation were purely practical—jointly they could produce what neither of them would have been able to produce alone—and this *practical argument* applies to peer production in general. With peer production, you don't have to wait for some market player to offer a solution that more or less tightly fits your problem, and you don't need all the capital, planning, determination, and luck that is necessary to successfully produce and sell your own solutions on the market. All you need is a group of other people who have problems or desires similar to your own, and the realization that it makes more sense for you to cooperate than to compete, and you are ready to go.

That joint production can be fun, that it can be deeply enjoyable and satisfying, is probably known to everyone who has ever tried it. The most famous representative of this *fun argument* is Linus Torvalds, the primary author of the *Linux kernel*[3], who entitled his autobiography "Just for Fun" (Torvalds and Diamond, 2001).

In capitalism, work is seldom fun—so seldom, in fact, that the conception that work and fun are opposites has become deeply ingrained in people's minds. In peer production, this antagonism is absent. While activities are not always pure fun,

---

[1] http://www.apache.org/

[2] http://httpd.apache.org/

[3] http://www.kernel.org/

they never become the dull drudgery of capitalism (if only because you know *why* you are doing something). Moreover, with the proposed task auctioning systems, everybody will be able to choose their preferred activities without having to feel remorse for imposing the less agreeable activities on others. This will probably make the open, cooperative and self-determined style of peer production even more enjoyable and fulfilling than it already is.

We suppose that the power of these arguments will be too strong for people to resist, at least in the long run. And we would not be surprised if many of the people getting first involved will come from two groups: Those who are worst off in the current system—because the new mode of production offers them chances that they don't have in the old one. And those who are very well off—because they have time and energy to spend on interesting new things, and peer production is the most interesting, challenging, and fun thing around, better than anything the traditional economy has to offer. Together, and together with everyone else who is sick or bored of the market or who wants to try a new and better mode of production, they might become a strong alliance.

Of course, these concluding remarks are mere speculations (though speculations based on arguments), since the future has not yet been written. How society will actually evolve depends on people's choices and actions—mine, yours, and everybody's. The future depends on us.

Bibliography

Michael Albert. *Parecon: Life After Capitalism.* Verso, London, 2004.

Christopher Alexander, Sara Ishikawa, Murray Silverstein, Max Jacobson, Ingrid Fiksdahl-King, and Shlomo Angel. *A Pattern Language: Towns, Buildings, Construction.* Oxford University Press, New York, 1977.

Apache Software Foundation. *About the Apache HTTP Server Project*, 2005. URL http://httpd.apache.org/ABOUT_APACHE.html. Accessed 2 May 2007.

Yochai Benkler. Coase's penguin, or, Linux and *The Nature of the Firm*. *The Yale Law Journal*, 112(3):369–446, 2002.

Yochai Benkler. *The Wealth of Networks: How Social Production Transforms Markets and Freedom.* Yale University Press, New Haven, Connecticut, 2006.

Neil A. Gershenfeld. *FAB: The Coming Revolution on Your Desktop—From Personal Computers to Personal Fabrication.* Basic Books, New York, 2005.

Pekka Himanen. *The Hacker Ethic and the Spirit of the Information Age.* Random House, New York, 2001. With a Prologue by Linus Torvalds.

John Holt. *Learning All the Time.* Perseus, Cambridge, MA, 1989.

Neil Hopkinson, Richard Hague, and Philip Dickens, editors. *Rapid Manufacturing: An Industrial Revolution for the Digital Age*. Wiley, Hoboken, NJ, 2006.

IETF. *RFC 2418: IETF Working Group Guidelines and Procedures*, 1998. URL http://tools.ietf.org/html/rfc2418. Accessed 2 May 2007.

Karim R. Lakhani and Robert G. Wolf. Why hackers do what they do: Understanding motivation and effort in free/open source software projects. In Joseph Feller, Brian Fitzgerald, Scott A. Hissam, and Karim R. Lakhani, editors, *Perspectives on Free and Open Source Software*. MIT Press, Cambridge, MA, 2005.

Frauke Lehmann. FLOSS developers as a social formation. *First Monday*, 9(11), 2004. URL http://www.firstmonday.org/issues/issue9_11/lehmann/index.html. Accessed 2 May 2007.

National Academy of Engineering. *Agricultural Mechanization – History part 4*, 2007. URL http://www.greatachievements.org/?id=3821. Accessed 2 May 2007.

Eric Steven Raymond. The cathedral and the bazaar. In *The Cathedral and the Bazaar: Musings on Linux and Open Source by an Accidental Revolutionary*. O'Reilly, Sebastopol, CA, 2nd edition, 2001.

Marshall Sahlins. *Stone Age Economics*. Tavistock, London, 1974.

Charles M. Schweik and Robert English. Tragedy of the FOSS commons? Investigating the institutional designs of free/libre and open source software projects. *First Monday*, 12(2), 2007. URL http://www.firstmonday.org/issues/issue12_2/schweik/index.html. Accessed 2 May 2007.

Richard M. Stallman. *Free Software, Free Society*. GNU Press, Boston, MA, 2002.

Linus Torvalds and David Diamond. *Just for Fun: The Story of an Accidental Revolutionary*. HarperCollins, New York, 2001.

Wikipedia. *Elegance*, 2007. URL http://en.wikipedia.org/wiki/Elegance. Accessed 2 May 2007.

Appendix

A. Mathematical Details of the Auctioning Models

This appendix is meant for people who are interested in some mathematical details of the proposed auctioning models. If you aren't, you can safely skip it. But don't be afraid—the used math is not hard, and it might help to better understand the models.

A.1. Task Auctioning

The purpose of task auctioning is to distribute the effort that is necessary to reach the goals of a project among all participants, in a way that is acceptable to all and that allows everybody to choose among the tasks they are able and willing to do according to their own preferences.

The effort E_t of a task t depends on two factors: the actual or estimated time T_t that it takes to complete the task, and the *labor weight* L_t that measures the popularity of this kind of task (labor):

$$E_t = T_t \times L_t \qquad \text{(A.1)}$$

All tasks are initially assumed to be equally popular, starting with $L_t = 1$. If there aren't enough suitable volunteers willing to do a task, its labor weight L_t is increased to make it more attractive (the same time spent for the task will now be recognized as a higher effort), until the number of volunteers ready to do the task under these more favorable conditions is sufficiently high. Conversely, if there are more volunteers than necessary, L_t is decreased until sufficiently many of them prefer to switch to different tasks that take less of their time (whose labor weight is higher).

How to put this auctioning system in practice? One way would be to use a *snapshot* model where all contributors select at once which tasks they are ready to do under which conditions (which lower limit of L_t they consider acceptable for each of them). The auction software then increases or decreases all $L_{t \in T}$ (T is the set of all tasks) simultaneously until it finds a configuration with the right number of volunteers for all tasks (if any exists). But this would require very conscious planning from the contributors since they would have to determine their preferences for all potentially suitable tasks at once, and there is no guarantee that a configuration matching all tasks with contributors exists.

Therefore an *iterative* model might be more suitable, where task assignment goes through multiple iterations. At each iteration, contributors decide which of the tasks $t \in T$ they are willing to handle assuming the current L_t values, and they specify a lower limit of L_t they consider acceptable for each of these tasks. If there are more contributors than required for a task t, the system automatically decreases the value of L_t until the number of contributors matches. But if there aren't enough contributors, the labor weight L_t is increased by no more than a specific amount (e.g., +2%), even if this means that there still aren't enough people willing to handle it.

This allows contributors to revise their preferences in the next iteration: those who have been dropped from their previous preferences (since the L_t value of a task has fallen below the lower limit they considered acceptable) now have to choose anew, stating their preferences as before but taking the updated L_t values into account. They might choose one of the not-yet-assigned "unpopular" tasks with a high L_t, or they might decide to accept a lower L_t limit for a previously selected task (which will cause the L_t of this task to fall even further). Each such iteration may take one day or some other suitable unit of time—it should not be *too* short to prevent the weight of unpopular tasks from increasing too quickly, but neither should it be too long so as not to heavily delay the execution of such tasks.

Such an iterative model is also suitable to take the natural fluctuation in any project into account—contributors will drop out and others will join, some tasks will be completed and new ones will arise, contributors will become bored of their activities and decide to try other ones. The weight of tasks will thus be constantly in flux—which will, of course, also influence the preferences of contributors.

How much effort will each contributor have to put into a project? This depends on the used allocation model (cf. Sec. 4.4.2). With *flat rates* (Sec. 4.4.2.1), the required summed effort $\sum_{t \in T} E_t$ is evenly shared among all contributors. If there are n contributors, each of them will have to contribute the same effort:

$$P = \frac{1}{n} \sum_{t \in T} E_t \qquad \textit{(flat rate)} \tag{A.2}$$

This is, in other words, the "price" to pay for getting access to the (non-copyable) products produced by the project.

With *flat allocation* (Sec. 4.4.2.2), the required effort does not depend on the number of contributors, but on the number of units produced. If there are m units, the price for each of them is

$$P = \frac{1}{m} \sum_{t \in T} E_t \qquad \textit{(flat allocation)} \tag{A.3}$$

The effort you have to contribute to the project thus depends on the number of units you want.

For the other allocation models (*production effort* and *preference weighting*), the relative effort required for producing a good needs to be taken into account. This will be covered in the next section.

A.2. Product Auctioning

E_x is the production effort that went into producing a good x, measured in weighted hours. $\sum_{x \in X} E_x$ is the summed production effort of all the goods produced by a project or distribution pool (X is the set of all produced goods). Note that $\sum_{x \in X} E_x = \sum_{t \in T} E_t$: the complete effort that goes into a project (or a whole distribution pool) stays of course the same, whether you slice it by produced goods or by tasks.

If accounting based on *production effort* (Sec. 4.4.2.3) is used, E_x is thus also the price of good x (i.e., the effort necessary to get it):

$$P_x = E_x \qquad \textit{(production effort)} \tag{A.4}$$

If *product auctioning* (Sec. 4.4.2.4) is used, the price of each product x is modified by an *allocation weight* A_x measuring the product popularity. Auctions start with $A_x = 1$. If there is more demand than can be satisfied, A_x is increased until the number of demands willing to accept the increased price matches the number of available products (*upward auctioning*). Conversely, if products have been produced that nobody wants, A_x can be decreased until there are sufficiently many persons willing to pick them up at the reduced price (*downward auctioning*).

With auctioning, a *normalization factor* N is necessary to ensure that the sum of efforts put into a project/distribution pool is equal to the summed price of its products:

$$\sum_{x \in X} E_x = \sum_{x \in X} P_x \tag{A.5}$$

The price of a product x is thus

$$P_x = A_x \times N \times E_x \qquad \textit{(product auctioning)} \tag{A.6}$$

N is calculated so as to ensure that the equation (A.5) holds:[1]

$$N = \frac{\sum_{x \in X} E_x}{\sum_{x \in X} (A_x \times E_x)} \tag{A.7}$$

Both upward auctioning and downward auctioning indicate that production should be adjusted to better meet the actual demand, if possible. However, there is a fundamental difference between upward and downward: in case of *upward* auctions, it is quite possible that production cannot be increased further (or at least not without negative side effects), due to a lack of required resources or space. However, *downward* auctioning signifies that it was a mistake to produce the product in question in the first place—nobody considers it worth the effort that has been necessary to produce it. (A mistake in so far as the good was produced for being *used*—its production might still be justified by the pleasure and satisfaction which the process of production gave to the producers.)

Of course, mistakes can occur (especially since prior esti-

[1] Proof that (A.7) fulfills equation (A.5):

$$\begin{aligned}
\sum_{x \in X} E_x &= \sum_{x \in X} P_x \\
&= \sum_{x \in X} (A_x \times N \times E_x) \\
&= N \times \sum_{x \in X} (A_x \times E_x) \\
&= \frac{\sum_{x \in X} E_x}{\sum_{x \in X} (A_x \times E_x)} \times \sum_{x \in X} (A_x \times E_x) \\
&= \sum_{x \in X} E_x
\end{aligned}$$

mations of the effort required for production will not always be exact), and downward auctioning is the best way to recover from them. However, downward auctions pose a specific problem for *distribution pools* (cf. Sec. 5.2). Since participating projects decide on their own what they want to produce, some of them could regularly produce things that are not "worth the effort," i.e., that require downward auctioning to be allocated. By doing so, they would raise the price for all the products produced within the distribution pool (since every $A_x < 1$ increases the value of the normalization factor N). Projects could even rip off the other pooling projects by producing goods nobody else is interested in and then acquiring them for a price below the production effort. This would allow the project members to use the difference between production effort and price ($\Delta_x = E_x - P_x$) to acquire other goods from the pool, without having contributed anything in return.

To avoid such situations (whether accidental or incidental), distribution pools will probably prefer to shift the risk of downward auctions to individual projects, by recognizing the required effort only partially, setting the *recognized effort*

$$R_x = \min(1, A_x) \times E_x \tag{A.8}$$

Thus, for products distributed at production effort or via upward auctioning ($A_x \geq 1$), the effort E_x is fully recognized as contribution, but in case of downward auctions ($A_x < 1$), the effort E_x is multiplied with the same weight A_x to derive the recognized effort R_x. This means that projects better take care that they produce products for which there is actual demand if they want to have all their efforts recognized.

The equation that a project or distribution pool has to fulfill to ensure that it gets enough contributions and that every contributor gets something in return now becomes

$$\sum_{x \in X} R_x = \sum_{x \in X} P_x \tag{A.9}$$

The normalization factor N needs to be modified accordingly:[2]

$$N = \frac{\sum_{x \in X} R_x}{\sum_{x \in X} (A_x \times E_x)} \tag{A.10}$$

Note that it will still be possible to acquire products for a price below the recognized production effort ($P_x < R_x$), due to the normalization factor N, which in this modified setup will always be ≤ 1 and usually (because of upward auctioning of some products) < 1.[3] This is not a problem—popular products being auctioned above production effort automatically reduces the price of all other products, since the additional effort necessary to acquire them needs to "go somewhere," and the only place where it can go is into the production of other products.

A.3. Resource Auctioning

Natural resources differ from products in requiring no human effort to produce them: $E_y = 0$ for all resources $y \in Y$, the set of available resources. When resources are made available in

[2] Proof that (A.10) fulfills equation (A.9): analogous to the proof that (A.7) fulfills (A.5).

[3] $R_x \leq (A_x \times E_x)$ holds for every $x \in X$:

$$\begin{aligned} R_x &= \min(1, A_x) \times E_x & &= A_x \times E_x \quad \text{if } A < 1 \textit{ (downward auctioning)} \\ R_x &= \min(1, A_x) \times E_x &= 1 \times E_x &= A_x \times E_x \quad \text{if } A = 1 \textit{ (production effort)} \\ R_x &= \min(1, A_x) \times E_x &= 1 \times E_x &< A_x \times E_x \quad \text{if } A > 1 \textit{ (upward auctioning)} \end{aligned}$$

Therefore, $N = \frac{\sum_{x \in X} R_x}{\sum_{x \in X} (A_x \times E_x)}$ will be 1 if upward auctioning is never used, and < 1 if it is used for some x.

a distribution pool in addition to products, the equation that needs to be fulfilled therefore becomes:

$$\sum_{x \in X} R_x = \sum_{x \in X} P_x + \sum_{y \in Y} P_y \tag{A.11}$$

Since resources don't take any production effort, but some of them will usually draw a non-zero price P_y, they will automatically decrease the price P_x of products.

For the same reason, there is no *upward* or *downward* auctioning of resources: since there is no production effort to recover, resource auctions can start with an initial price $P_y = 0$. If the demand for a resource is below or equal the available amount, every bidder gets the resource at this price, i.e., for free. Otherwise P_y is increased until the remaining demand matches the availability (the resulting P_y will be slightly higher than the highest bid that *cannot* be satisfied). Analogously to task and product auctions, it might be reasonable to use an *iterative* model, where unsuccessful bidders can re-estimate their valuation of the resource and increase their bid. The auction ends when the set of successful bidders hasn't changed during one iteration.

A.4. Virtual Effort

In the text we mentioned two instances where the people participating in distribution pools might decide to recognize *virtual effort*—effort that hasn't actually been spent but that can be used to acquire products and resources. Virtual effort may be granted to persons who are exempted from contributing (cf. Sec. 8.1.1) to allow them to get products and resources in the same way as contributors; and it may be granted to the locals of especially popular places where the auctioning of grounds and houses leads to increased prices (cf. Sec. 8.3.1).

Virtual effort makes people eligible for products and resources in the same way as actually contributed and recognized effort. Therefore, the summed price of products and resources must equal the sum of all recognized actual *and* all virtual effort. If V_e is the virtual effort a person e is eligible for, and E is the set of all eligible people, equation (A.11) must be modified as follows:

$$\sum_{x \in X} R_x + \sum_{e \in E} V_e = \sum_{x \in X} P_x + \sum_{y \in Y} P_y \qquad \text{(A.12)}$$

The actual size of $\sum_{e \in E} V_e$ depends on the conditions of granting virtual effort. Above (Sec. 8.1.1) we discussed two models of granting virtual effort to persons exempted from contributing. The first was to consider non-contributors as "average" contributors. Thus, we have to splice the recognized effort contributed to a distribution pool by contributors $c \in C$, instead of by produced goods $x \in X$ or by required tasks $t \in T$. Of course, this does not change the effort itself:

$$\sum_{c \in C} R_c = \sum_{x \in X} R_x = \sum_{t \in T} R_t \qquad \text{(A.13)}$$

The *average* recognized effort is $\bar{R}_C = \frac{1}{|C|} \sum_{c \in C} R_c$, where $|C|$ is the size of the set C, i.e., the number of contributors. This average will be granted as virtual effort to each non-contributor eligible for this scheme:

$$V_e = \bar{R}_C = \frac{1}{|C|} \sum_{c \in C} R_c \qquad \textit{(contributor average)} \qquad \text{(A.14)}$$

The discussed alternative was to entitle each ex-contributor to virtual effort equivalent to her *personal* recognized contributions averaged over her active years (or over a subset of them, say the last ten years). If $R_{e_1}, R_{e_2}, \ldots, R_{e_n}$ is the recognized effort contributed by e during the n relevant years, and if this second scheme is used, the virtual effort to which e will be entitled will be her personal average over these years:

$$V_e = \bar{R}_e = \frac{1}{n} \sum_{i=1}^{n} R_{e_i} \qquad \textit{(personal average)} \qquad \text{(A.15)}$$

For people who have never contributed anything, such as children and other people fulfilling some exemption criterion since their birth, only the first scheme will be possible. The second might be more suitable for ex-contributors: people who have contributed in the past but cannot any longer, e.g., due to old age or illness. Of course, the local associations participating in a distribution pool might decide to use other schemes, for example to grant each ex-contributor the *maximum* of the contributor average and her personal average, i.e., to apply the scheme which leads to more virtual effort being granted.

The second instance where we mentioned virtual effort concerned the auctioning of grounds and houses as a regulation mechanism for migration (Sec. 8.3.1). The open auction of grounds and houses in a distribution pool will lead to higher prices in popular places, therefore reducing their attractiveness for potential immigrants and mitigating their risk of becoming overcrowded—but it likewise affects the people who have been born there and want to stay. This can be partially compensated by calculating how much *additional* effort the locals of a community have to spend due to their community being popular, and to give (say) half of this effort back as virtual effort. Thus they would only have to make actual contributions for half of the additional effort required, while the other half is unconditionally granted to them.

To arrange such a scheme it will be necessary to first define who is a *local*. A sensible way of doing so would be to regard as *locals* of any specific local community all the people who lived there several years ago (e.g., five years ago), regardless of whether they still live there or whether they have moved elsewhere. In this way, immigrants won't be considered as immigrants forever (which would be hard to justify), but will automatically become locals after some years.

Second, it is necessary to find out how much additional effort (if any) the locals of a community have to spend due to the open auctioning of the grounds and houses in their area. This can be done by complementing the actual auctioning of grounds and houses with a *shadow auction* where only the bids of locals are considered. Let P_{GH} be the summed price of all grounds and houses situated in a local community in the actual auction; and P^*_{GH} the summed price that would have resulted for these grounds and houses in the shadow auction. We can now determine whether the locals of the respective community have to pay higher prices for being popular by calculating

$$\Delta_{GH} = P_{GH} - P^*_{GH} \qquad \text{(A.16)}$$

Since the shadow auction simulates the fictitious situation that no migration takes place, it will also need to include bids from locals that in reality have moved elsewhere (and hence are no longer bidding). This can be done by repeating the last bids that locals made prior to moving away.

If Δ_{GH} is positive, the locals did have to spend additional effort due to the popularity of their community. If 50% of this effort are given back to the locals and if there are n locals, the virtual effort granted to each local e of the concerned local community will be

$$V_e = \frac{0.5}{n}\Delta_{GH} \qquad \textit{(local of popular community)} \qquad \text{(A.17)}$$

(Of course, if *e* happens to be exempted, she will additionally be granted virtual effort due to her personal or the contributor average as discussed above.)

It makes sense to distribute this virtual effort among *all* the locals of a community, regardless of where they live now. Otherwise people would be disadvantaged by moving from one local community to another one of similar popularity (maybe just the neighboring community), which would unnecessarily impede migration. Always granting people the virtual effort due to the locals of the community where they lived five years ago will encourage people to move from popular to less popular places, and it will cause people to think twice before they move in the other direction. Thus it will counteract the "natural" popularity of different places, just as intended.

About the Author

Dr. **Christian Siefkes** is a co-founder of the German-language Freie-Gesellschaft-Wiki[1] and Keimform-Blog[2], a wiki and a blog dedicated to some of the questions investigated in this text. His prior involvements with the free software community include translations for the GNU Project[3] and contributions to the spam filtering community which influenced free spam filters such as CRM114[4] and OSBF-Lua[5]. Christian Siefkes holds a Ph.D. in computer science from the Freie Universität, Berlin, Germany, and is currently working as a freelance software engineer and text mining expert.
Web: http://www.siefkes.net/; e-mail: christian [at] siefkes [dot] net.

Acknowledgments

This text would not exist without numerous intense discussions and long evenings with Andreas F. Hoffmann, Frauke Lehmann, Holger Weiß, Kurt Jansson, and the other members of the Berlin discussion group on "Free Software, Free Knowledge, Free Society." I also want to thank Benni Bärmann, Stefan Meretz, Thomas Kalka, and the other participants of the Keimform-Blog and the Freie-Gesellschaft-Wiki, as well as Martin Siefkes and Matthias Fischmann, for inspiration and fruitful debates.

---

1 http://www.freie-gesellschaft.de/
2 http://www.keimform.de/
3 http://www.gnu.org/
4 http://crm114.sourceforge.net/
5 http://osbf-lua.luaforge.net/

www.ingramcontent.com/pod-product-compliance
Lightning Source LLC
Chambersburg PA
CBHW032001040426
42448CB00006B/449

* 9 7 8 3 9 4 0 7 3 6 0 0 0 *